DISTANT SUMMERS

Philip Casey by Eamonn Carter

For All our Distant Summers
Steps of Damer, Dublin June 27, 2007

DISTANT SUMMERS
Remembering Philip Casey
Writer, Fabulist, Friend

Eamonn Wall, Katie Donovan, Michael Considine
EDITORS

ARLEN
HOUSE

Distant Summers
Remembering Philip Casey

is published in 2024 by

ARLEN HOUSE
42 Grange Abbey Road
Baldoyle
Dublin 13
Ireland
Phone: 00 353 86 8360236
arlenhouse@gmail.com
www.arlenhouse.ie

978–1–85132–314–2, *paperback*

Distributed internationally by
SYRACUSE UNIVERSITY PRESS
621 Skytop Road, Suite 110
Syracuse
NY 13244–5290
USA
Phone: 315–443–5534
supress@syr.edu
syracuseuniversitypress.syr.edu

Typesetting by Arlen House

cover image:
photograph of Philip Casey
courtesy of the Casey family

CONTENTS

INTRODUCTION

Eamonn Wall, Katie Donovan, Michael Considine

As the pandemic began to ebb and the flow of ordinary life resumed, a plan began to form among the three of us – all old friends and admirers of Philip Casey, with similar roots in Wexford. It was time. Time to present readers with a collection that would serve as a tribute to this much-missed writer and unique friend. For the past two years, we have met in person and via Zoom to plot, talk, imagine, and project. Though we knew that Philip Casey's work was widely read and that many loved him as a person, we were still, nonetheless, amazed by the response to our call for submissions.

As a reader of this collection, you will be taken on a journey. The book that you are holding in your hands contains personal essays, poems, literary criticism, paintings, and photographs all exploring aspects of Philip Casey's life and work. We have included selections from his published work: poetry, and fiction for both adults and children. In addition, we are publishing for the first time extracts from Philip's unpublished *Histories of the Irish*, the work that preoccupied him for the last decade of his life. Also, *Distant Summers* includes an extensive and detailed bibliography of Philip's published work in various formats: book, journal, newspaper, and digital. This will be an invaluable resource for anyone who wishes to do research on Philip's work.

We are confident that people will continue to read Philip Casey. A reader wandering through a bookshop somewhere will have her eye caught, for example, by the lustrous blue cover of *The Water Star*. She will reach for it, leaf through it, then take it home with her to read and savour. Later, she will return to the same bookshop

Bann River Trilogy

seeking the other novels that make up the Bann River Trilogy: *The Fabulists* and *The Fisher Child*. She will tell her friends about the discovery she has made. When books excite us, we want others to join in.

Elsewhere, in a public library a young man will come across a copy of *The Year of the Knife*, one of Philip's collections of poetry. Transfixed in the aisle and rooted there, he will slowly read the poems, his eyes lit by the wonder of the language and the depth of the vision. He takes this book home and seeks a quiet place to read. He will find that the poems are speaking to him, that they seem to be poems written for him and for no other person. "Philip Casey," this young man will intone. "I want to know more about this man and his work."

Future readers will quickly learn what we already know – that Philip Casey was and is an incomparable literary talent whose work lingers in the mind long after it has been read, and the book set aside.

Distant Summers is a work of many voices that offers readers unique insights into the world that Philip Casey inhabited and graced until his untimely death in 2018. We learn from the essays contributed by his siblings what it was like to grow up with Philip during his early years in London and on the family farm in Hollyfort, County Wexford, that period of his life when his imaginative and ethical life was being formed. They describe his illnesses and hospitalisations and how he suffered and endured guided by a mixture of optimism, humour and stoicism. They remind us that not only was Philip admired as a writer and friend, but he was also loved and idolised as brother.

In addition to family members, the contributors to this volume form a pantheon of his peers and contemporary Irish writers. Each individual who crossed paths with Philip and has written for this volume was left with a bright and positive mark. While everyone acknowledges the enduring sense of loss they feel now that Philip no longer lives among us, all attest to how genuine he was and to the great quality of his work. Some think more highly of Philip's work as a poet while others stand firmly by his fiction. Everyone remembers Philip's warm and booming laugh and how firm his handshake was.

Philip was one of a generation of writers from Wexford who came together under the guiding light of James Liddy and Paul Funge to give readings at the Gorey Arts Festival, and publish our writing in *The Gorey Detail* which Liddy edited with such aplomb in the 1970s and 1980s. We remember those exhilarating early days of finding our voices and finding an audience. Philip, ever a generous mentor to other writers, was at the heart of this scene.

Distant Summers is also a pocket literary history of Dublin from the earliest days of Raven Arts Press to the present. While staying in close and loyal contact with his roots in County Wexford, Philip made his home on Arran Street East, near the Four Courts and the Fruit Market. Many of the contributors to this book made the journey there to meet him and talk with him in his book-lined front room. He lived on a quiet street in the middle of a busy city, a steady mind in the midst of the world's storms. Philip Casey grew to become a consummate Dublin writer who chronicled the city in great depth in his poetry and in his first novel *The Fabulists*. Another focus we have included in this compendium is Philip's embrace of the new technologies and digital media that led him to create and curate Irish Writers Online and eMaker Editions.

We are grateful to the writers and friends of Philip who have contributed to this volume, and for the advice and encouragement they have offered. Thanks to the Casey family for their encouragement and support and for sharing their own stories of Philip, many of which are new to us. We are grateful to everyone who has subscribed to this volume: you have made it possible. Finally, great thanks to Alan Hayes of Arlen House for his enthusiasm for this project, one derived from his own admiration for Philip Casey and love of his work.

DISTANT SUMMERS

Robert Armstrong

Deep Valley

1993, oil on canvas, 91 x 71cm

(l to R) *Eamonn Carter, Lorcan Brennan, Paddy Kehoe, Philip Casey, Jim Chapson, Michael Considine, Liam O'Connor, Eamonn Wall, James Liddy and Paul Funge*

The photo was for a cover of *The Gorey Detail*. I used to art direct these back in the day and Tony Murray was the photographer. The concept was based on *The Anatomy Lesson of Dr. Nicolaes Tulp*, one of Rembrandt's most impressive group portraits.

Michael Augustin

MEMORIAL SERVICE, MOUNT JEROME

Your crutches, Philip
displayed in front of all of us
gathered here

Your crutches, Philip
daffodil yellow, blue cuffs and grips
blackish brown rubberized feet

Your crutches, Philip
unable to walk the streets of Dublin
without you

As w/ any anthology, there is a
mixture of talent & ability on display
— which in many ways is part of its charm.

Sebastian Barry, Philip and Antony Farrell, publisher, Lilliput Press, at the launch of The Fabulists

Michael Augustin, Philip and Sujuta Bhatt

Sebastian Barry

My Philip

Ah dear Philip, where do you abide? Our little world is getting worse and worse, we're told, and many of the things that troubled you, and that you touched on in your writing so artfully, would trouble you even more now. Since you had had your own personal vicissitudes, even as a child, you wished vicissitudes on no one. Your heart was encompassing, far-reaching, immense. A Goreyman, you imaginatively roamed the world. Well, not straight away Gorey, England first, as a small boy. You took the trouble to do that very Irish thing, be born elsewhere, and bring your Irishness home like owls to Athens. Your mother gorged you on library books, as a growing boy you knew far more than most, and noticed everything with a doubting appetite. Like Kavanagh before you, you were 'king of every blooming thing'. Illness shook you, bedevilled you, was reluctant ever to let you go, right to the end, and back to the beginning. I always saw you in heroic terms, because you never did so yourself. You hated, hated hospital because you knew it would suck you into its systems for months and months, and threaten never to let you return to what you wanted to be – a fine literary person, in a small house near the river Liffey, that your father had helped you buy. There to write, and walk about the city, and be visited and loved by your friends. A simple life, infinitely hard to attain. You attained it. What sort of person never talks ill of another, ever, even when strained to the very limits of their kindness and patience? Well, Philip, you might not have liked me saying so, but a sort of secular saint is the answer, which is what you were, definitely – some sort of holy man, anyway, Philip, forgive me for saying it out loud.

Do you remember the first time we bumped into each other? You had amazingly (when all others had more or less condemned) written a kind review of a crazyish book of mine, so when I sighted you I didn't fear to say hello. You repeated your praise of a long poem in particular that had annoyed everyone else. I suppose maybe you did hold those views, but there was an important instinct in you that knew that criticism, even when deserved, could be ridiculously and destructively painful. You had intuited a vicissitude. You were of a mind to take it away. The kindness of a stranger, but also, a fellow writer. Truly a fellow writer. In this also, an adroit hero, in the Homeric and Virgilian sense.

So, a friendship, dating from 1986, about the time I met Alison, my other comrade-in-arms, whom you adored, and who adored you. Over you would traipse on your jazzy crutches through the dark nights and bright nights of an Irish year, to North Great George's Street, 'before the twins were born', when we had time to talk and shoot the cuff, and cook up eggs, beans and chips, your kind of dinner, any sensible person's kind of dinner. You often spoke of things that the amazed listener might have thought had been the preserve of their own private minds. Of ethics, politics, friendships, poems. You knew you were a poet, the first requisite of being one. You took enormous pleasure in the deeply affirmative act of writing a poem. When one flew in on mysterious wings, you knew it was on the borders of the miraculous, and what's more you had awaited its coming with immense patience. As for the ordinary vicissitudes of being young, and trying to make your way, you borrowed humorously a phrase from another branch of Irish life entirely, *tiocfaidh ár lá*.

And your day did come, many times, you got your novels published and your poems printed, you won your prizes with a quiet satisfaction. Member of Aosdána! Perhaps you had been so deeply affrighted as a child by illness, that the little terrors of the literary life didn't affect you too much. But the triumphs certainly delighted you, as did so many things in the passing parade of your life. You were an absolute connoisseur of the so-called ordinary, which is nothing of the sort. Those summer mornings in Dublin when every denizen is equalised by the lambent light. The matchless pleasure of seeing a friend after a long absence. Countless things. Did ever a person live with greater poise, to greater purpose, with an adroitness and a dancingness that mere crutches couldn't alter? Well, perhaps, but only in a brotherhood and sisterhood of angels.

In later years Alison and myself were much preoccupied with the children and we moved away from Dublin and so saw you less. But now and then we retouched the friendship, like a fine old painting. And I am so glad I followed an instinct and went in to see you that last time, when all you spoke of was the work you still were going to do, *had* to do, a history of Ireland no less, and why not, and all your care was to calm your foolish visitor, allowing us to part as we had met, as deep friends. My Philip!

I am giving you a character reference of a sort for any possible St Peter, though you hardly need it now. Can you hear me through the moils and distances of the great heavens? You knew infinitely more than I did when you were alive and now you know everything. You have outstripped even yourself. You have found the end of the rainbow in some familiar Wexford field, bagged up the gold, and tamed the unicorn.

Sara Berkeley

GENTLY, GENTLY, GENTLENESS

In June 1983, when I was sixteen, I sent a sheaf of poems to Dermot Bolger. He had formed Raven Arts Press six years before at the age of seventeen. Raven was based on the simple idea that the workers seize the means of production, so that although Dermot was publisher and Philip and several others editors, they were all primarily poets. I'd get the 17a after school to the Raven offices on North Great Frederick Street where Dermot and Philip would sit in the front room surrounded by boxes of books and go over my poems with me.

You couldn't wish for a gentler, kinder, more generous editor than Philip Casey. He and Dermot plied me with the books Raven was publishing, a heady collection of Francis Stuart, Michael O'Loughlin, Paul Durcan, Conleth O'Connor, and the two of them. Raised on a school diet of Yeats and Kavanagh, Philip's work impressed me with its urban edge. He was writing of drunks on the Liffey's bridges, the bakery hard by the markets, and dole queues. He opened my eyes to Europe – East Berlin, Hamburg, southern Spain – and to figures like Rosa Luxembourg and Frida Kahlo. His poetry was hard-hitting, visceral, unabashed. But in our exchanges, there was nothing but kindness and a wicked humour.

Philip was a master of deflecting limelight from himself. He inscribed my copy of *After Thunder* 'for Sara, nice to have you home in my book, Love Philip'. I would have had no idea what he meant had he not shown me with an asterisk that my name appeared on the opposite page under 'Recent Books from Raven'. His poetry gave glimpses into the *sleepless reich of phantom pain* in which he lived, the nights in a hospital bed. In person, he never mentioned them.

They were wild years, and he and Dermot seemed afraid of leading me astray, schoolgirl that I was. In a postcard from Annaghmakerrig in 1985, Dermot warned me:

> on no account should you ignore your studies and go to the Winding Stair on Thursday the 10th, where a lot of gits will be launching Philip Casey's book, drinking cheap wine and misbehaving.

When they were publishing *After the War is Over* in response to Reagan's 1984 visit to Ireland, they suggested I discuss the book with my mother before agreeing to have a poem included. As if I, at seventeen, would have turned down the chance to be published alongside some of Ireland's foremost poets!

Most of my memories of Philip are from these years, when he still had the sidies and the mop of dark hair. Our readings were in pubs and urban libraries and, always, the Winding Stair. Raven moved from North Frederick Street to above a Finglas betting office. We typed each other letters on tissuey paper. Philip was a constant, thorough, kind editorial guide for my work. His wry humour in our editorial sessions reminded me not to take life too seriously. His natural shying from attention matched my model for how I wanted to be as a writer in the world.

I had been many years in California when I got the news of his death. It sent me back to an old poem of his from the late 1980s, 'Making Space'. It's a testament to his signature generosity, a lovely notion that his legacy would be nothing more or less than a light for us to read by in the night.

Philip Casey

MAKING SPACE

Sometimes, when looking at the stars
on a clear night in summer,

I wonder about light
and the energy that keeps me upright.
What does the Principle
of the Conservation of Energy
say, and does it apply to me,
and when I die
will I be transformed into a thought
travelling at the speed of light?

Perhaps, you will turn me on at the flick
of a switch, to bathe your smile
while you nod off over a book.
My light and how lovely you look
will describe a time and place
as you reach out, making space
in your calm sleep
for your lost black sheep
whose molecules keep your bedroom lit.
I will burn for you all night.

Sujata Bhatt

SOUTH OF THE ELBE
for Philip Casey, who knew the Elbe well

East of the Elbe lives the hooded crow.
West of the Elbe, the carrion crow.

I have travelled from East to West
and back again from West to East.
I have travelled endlessly.

All morning I watched these hooded crows:
how slender they are, how elegant
beneath the tall pine trees.
The pine trees are also slender
and the wind makes them sway so easily.
Sometimes it seems as if that's all they want to do:
just sway from side to side
while the crows flick through pine needles and grass.

I can watch the light for days,
how it moves between the crows and the trees.

My mind wanders:
The hooded crows take me back
to Maninagar –
the pine trees to Maine.

Now this poem could go almost anywhere.

Philip with Dermot Bolger, his first publisher, the Mansion House, 2015

Dermot Bolger

EULOGY FOR PHILIP

I was privileged to be asked by Philip's family to make a short speech at his funeral in Mount Jerome on the 8th of February in 2017. I have vivid memories of that service in Mount Jerome, and of many other moments in the year which led up to his death. I recall the Mount Jerome ceremony as not just the day on which I said farewell to one of my oldest and closest friends in Philip, but also as the last occasion on which I met his great friend and mine, the poet Matthew Sweeney. Despite being seriously ill himself, Matthew had bravely travelled to Dublin to be there.

The previous night – in the funeral home where Philip was being waked – was the last occasion when I saw Philip's childhood friend from their shared time in Cappagh Hospital, the writer Paddy Doyle, distraught in his wheelchair beside the open coffin of his close friend. Paddy's book, *The God Squad*, might never have seen printer's ink – and played its part in transforming Ireland by being the first book to lift the lid on childhood institutional abuse – if Philip had not quietly but firmly pressed the manuscript into my hands, with the simple words, "this story needs to be told". This was back in 1988, after bigger publishers than my tiny Raven Arts Press had shied away from its dangerous truths. But this was Philip's way, always discreetly matchmaking behind the scenes, resolute in his belief that certain voices must be heard and certain truths told.

At that ceremony in Mount Jerome, I recalled my memories of first shaking hands with Philip forty years before, at a vibrant arts festival in Gorey. I joked to the gathering of family and friends it was that only now, four decades on, that some small semblance of feeling was returning to my crushed fingers. And I went on to say:

"When you shook hands with Philip, his grip was so tight that your hand stayed shook. His handshake was as unforgettable as his laughter; as unforgettable as his infectious warmth; his hospitality; his generosity of spirit; his razor-sharp, cosmopolitan intellectual curiosity about politics and social matters; his human interest in how you were (and his deflection of talk away from his own pain in later years, the only hint of which was in the lines on his face); his deft duality in being a true citizen of cities – Dublin, Barcelona, Hamburg or Berlin, and also in being a proudly unreconstructed Wexford yellow belly – which is my own antecedence too.

In his work and talk, Philip showed his deep love of the Wexford people he grew up among – as part of the close, loving family he was so proud of. And as a true farmer's son he possessed no shred of sentimentality towards the realities of rural life.

Philip was a citizen of everywhere and a true poet of everywhere, whether in his Wexford poems or the Dublin he made his own in *The Fabulists*; or the bombed-out London streets of his early childhood conjured up in *The Water Star*, or the 1798 Rebellion in Wexford and slave plantations of Montserrat brilliantly evoked in *The Fisher Child*.

While his novels are superb, Philip will be remembered primarily as a poet. Since his passing so many people have mentioned how certain poems of his opened up journeys for them into their own souls. But while his colleagues, friends and readers will remember his gift for words, we will also remember something equally precious and rare: his great and unique gift for friendship. We remember Philip as a beacon of light and his small quayside house as an ark.

When you are young there are places like your parents' home where you know that you will always be welcome, with no need to explain yourself. For hundreds of us, Philip's house became such an ark and sanctuary, no matter what age we were.

He was the greatest of friends, the greatest of listeners, a man whose presence you never left without being buoyed by his warmth and grace, without walking away, feeling taller and renewed because you had been blessed by the benediction and sacrament of his friendship.

As an unlapsed agnostic, this is a metaphor Philip might tut-tut against with his amused smile, but the truth is, as his great friend, Sebastian Barry, said to me on the night that he died, *Maybe Philip was just one of those angels that we apparently don't believe in.*

I feel uniquely bereaved at having lost one of my closest, most special friends with whom I shared a unique, irreplaceable friendship. Yet I know that I am not unique here: that those same words could apply to half of the people present here today.

Each of our friendships with Philip was unique because he was unique. Without him being aware of his specialness, he made us feel unique by allowing us to share in our aura, his essence of goodness and of greatness, his love of words in his poems that will live on in the minds of readers who truly appreciate poetry and in his greater love of family and friends – a love too that will never die for so long as any of us remain alive to still feel that warmth and grace he left lodged in our hearts.

As fellow writers, readers, neighbours, friends, we may not have said it often enough, and many of us never have had a chance to say it at the end when he was in the hospice. So while I cannot claim to speak for anyone, I feel I speak for many here when I say, this one last time, goodbye old pal; thank you for blessing us with your life, your poems and with your friendship."

I can still hear his laugh, still recall the steadfast firmness of his handshake, and recall too, the steadfast integrity of this man whom I, and so many others, were blessed to be able to call our friend.

Pat Boran

THIS IS A BOOK
i.m. Philip Casey

This is a book. It is what happens
when the batteries die, when the lights
go out, when the wires that join the world
into the fantasy of connectedness
run cold. Somewhere, somewhen,
a man sat down, a woman cleared
a space in the riot of a sunlit room
or lamplit cave, a hospital bed
or the rocking bunk of a boat far out
at sea – and began to dream.
This book, and the words it was made
to protect, came later, and was far
from guaranteed. And even now, who knows –
and this is the dream of every book –
a talking dog or walking table,
a land of such great beauty the gods
require two suns to do it justice,
comes to life and lives each time
these words made of ink like tiny plants
respond to the light, when a passing breeze
or a breath turns over the page.

The first time I met Philip Casey, I embarrassed him so much that I think he did his best to avoid me for the following few days. Thereafter we became good friends.

It was late 1985 and I'd just moved into a bedsit in a house on Longwood Avenue, off Dublin's South Circular Road. That I had come to live in that particular house after routinely answering an advert in the classifieds section of the *Irish Press* seems unlikely now, but that's how it was.

No plan, just the strings of fate drawing me along. Little did I know the day I moved in that on the floor above me was the painter Sean Fingleton and, below me in the basement, the poet Philip Casey, neither of whom I had met before, though, as it happens, I knew something about the work of each.

Though I was living in Dublin only a few years at the time, I'd already fallen in with a small group of artists and writers and, as I got to know my way around the Dublin scene, I paid particular attention any time I heard positive references to a practitioner working outside of the group (not always a daily occurrence!) Many people I met enthused about the energy and commitment of the painter Fingleton (about his powerful, troubled landscapes that seemed to have been wrestled onto the canvas), but they seemed to have a special reverence for Philip Casey which made me keen to meet him.

Coming and going with my bags of vegetables from the stalls on Camden Street, or a collection of wooden scraps gathered for my open fire from the skips along the canal in Portobello (gentrification was already in full swing), in that first week or so I'd take my time on the steps up to the front door of Longwood Avenue, hoping for a glimpse of the basement poet I was too shy to disturb.

And then one morning, without warning, as I came down to head out on some errand or other, there was a noise from below and behind, and I turned around to see the basement door open and a small (to me) man leaning on a crutch emerging. It was Philip Casey.

I was in the grip of an enthusiastic apprenticeship to poetry, and reading everything I could get my hands on, including *After Thunder*, his poetry collection that had come out only months before. I told him so. Philip smiled warily. I really liked it. He thanked me politely. Neither of us moved. In an effort to put him at his ease, and to relieve my own growing sense of discomfort, I mentioned a few people we had in common – the poets Leland Bardwell and Pearse Hutchinson, Tommy Smith, the owner and heart of Grogan's Castle Lounge, then effectively my home from home.

And then I did the unthinkable. I named one of the poems from Philip's book. 'Machine Buried', for some reason, had made a particular impression on me when I first read it not long before, so much so that in a period where I had more free time than now (and a significantly better memory), standing there in the shadow of the house I began to recite the entire thing to him from memory: 'The early shift poured into the works,/some hungover, faces drawn and eyes/sleep-caked, sleep-heavy, their mood morose,/unready for its troubling presence ...' And Philip just stood there and looked at me, in shock, in wonder, radiating his typical kindness and concern.

Sensing I was trying too hard, I stopped halfway through, and we exchanged a few pleasantries and promised to get together for a chat one day. And then we scurried off, each in his own direction, wisely choosing the neutral territory of a bar or coffee shop for our next encounter, before which I had already begun to understand something important about poets. The true ones are always surprised when anyone reads, let alone memorises their work. They give all they have in its making, but then step away from it and leave it to find its own way in the world. They hope their poems will live beyond them, but fear deep down no such thing will ever happen.

Philip endured more suffering than almost anyone I've known, and not just once but again and again. Yet he never complained, and he never gave up making new things, poems and novels, and helping and encouraging others to make their own as well.

There are plenty of poems by Philip that move me more than does 'Machine Buried'; there are things about this fable of men at work that I still don't entirely understand or can't apply to the man I got to know over the many years since. And, in truth, it wasn't a poem Philip himself made any great claim for or returned to often. Perhaps he remained puzzled about it, as poets often are about their work.

But something in it made great sense, haunted and inspired the young writer I was back then trying to become. And that's why I turn to it again today, as we say goodbye to Philip and have only the poems and the novels in his place (with all the pressure that puts on them now). I turn to it again because there are mysteries in poems, and in poem-making, that cannot be explained away, that always seem to have something more to tell us, something more to reveal. We lose our loves and our friends, but something we write as in a dream, or stumble upon by accident in a public library on a rainy afternoon, becomes our farewell message to the world, and someone's lifelong companion.

Philip Casey

MACHINE BURIED

The early shift poured into the works,
some hungover, faces drawn and eyes
sleep-caked, sleep-heavy, their mood morose,
unready for its troubling presence.
It had taken root in the concrete,
a steel Zeus from a mouthful of dust.
Wary, they searched it for a device
that might breathe some life into its steel,
but it was inert and they withdrew,
disconcerted, and deep in their hearts,
afraid. As with the precursors of plagues,

it had come among them unannounced.
In heaven, alias the office,
all ranks were blissfully certain
that no such god existed, demi-
or other, there being no record.
The men returned to work
but in every mind lurked the machine,
which they had christened Colonel Blink.
Then came the solution from on high:
a hole was dug and as the bulldozer
toppled it over the brink, they stared,
feigning laughter; but true to his instinct
a mechanic sprinkled oil on its
complex extremities and they cheered.
The clay was expertly cemented
over, but each year it subsides just
a little and each time a man walks
across it he has a strange feeling,
like an old night-fear from childhood.

(from *After Thunder,* 1985)

Ulrike Boskamp

FOUR LOVING MEMORIES OF PHILIP CASEY

1982, Dublin – *love, dampness, hippies*

We fell in love in Philip's basement apartment in Longwood Avenue. Completely lost in love. I had arrived with a friend of Philip's one evening and left forever changed and hooked. We shared ideas and convictions that we never gave up (him less than me), and the intimacy of this kept us together for life. We visited a reading by Jacob Holdt who had published a photo book, *Bilder aus Amerika (Pictures from America)* a few years earlier, a book that seems to be forgotten today. Holdt had undertaken a hitchhike trip through the US, had accepted any lifts, accommodations, contacts, and sex that he was offered. With this openness to everything, he was and somewhat remained a soulmate of our shared convictions.

1990s, Berlin and Dublin – *transcultural experiences*

We visited back and forth between Dublin and Berlin regularly over 35 years, but we also met in London, Hamburg and Paris, and we took each other on trips through our respective countries. Philip regularly travelled to Germany. That resulted in the strange experience that my life, friends and stories became raw materials for his literary work. One precious shared summer memory was a day trip from Berlin to the river Oder with my reading group of seven female philosophers – to which Philip was admitted as a guest, a fact he remained proud of.

1999, Paris – *beauty and the love of technology*

I had a research grant to Paris. It was in the early days of mobile phones, and I had one, and I rang Philip. This resulted in an hour-long wandering through Paris in the spring sun, pure joy. I remember crossing the Seine, reporting on views and smells and sights, and how Philip enjoyed hearing my steps across Paris through the phone. How typical of him it was to appreciate and use the wonders of new technologies.

2014, Rathnew – *poetry and the future*
My daughter Klara and Philip very much enjoyed each other's company, each other's wit and sense of humour. One summer we were visiting Ireland, Klara was 13. I had left Philip and Klara in the garden of Hunter's Hotel. When I came back they were composing a song, after a curious, disconcerting, but also amusing shared experience: A man had broken out into roaring laughter while he was looking at them. We have a recording of them singing their song together:

The Laughing Man

I was sitting in the garden, reading a book,
drinking a tea,
and suddenly
a laughing man comes up to me!
O laughing man, o laughing man,
why are you laughing at me?
Is it my hair, is it my shirt, is it my eyes,
is it my teeth?
O laughing man, o laughing man,
why are you laughing at me?
Have you been drinking?
Cause that's what I've been thinking
O laughing man, o laughing man,
why are you laughing at me?

I was going down the street
the air was sweet, but who did I meet?

The laughing man!
O laughing man, o laughing man,
why are you laughing at me?
Is it my hair, is it my shirt, is it my eyes,
is it my teeth?
Have you been drinking?
That's what I've been thinking!
O laughing man, o laughing man,
why are you laughing at me?

Going in a shop
some pretty clothes I got,
nice boutique, but then I freaked!
O laughing man, the laughing man
was laughing at me!
O laughing man, o laughing man,
why are you laughing at me?
Is it my hair, is it my shirt, is it my eyes,
is it my teeth?

It's your shirt he says, your shirt he says,
the smiley on your shirt!

Philip, Ulrike Boskamp and Klara Boskamp on Arran Street East

Sean Halford

ANNAGH HILL

Lorcan Brennan

ANNAGH HILL
for Philip Casey

Up near the celestial viewing point
close to a ring of foxgloves

a lone rabbit has settled
for sleep, rested and free.

Late evening light
has brought its mystical
healing glaze

and all about, recovered anthems
from those distant summers
whisper out across our fields,
our counties, our friendships

their sacred calls of remembrance.

Heather Brett

Not an Obituary
A gift for Philip

I

Someday,
one of us will be informed of
the death of the other
and in that first long moment
when the world will seem to fall away
and it's just ourselves left, miniscule,
standing absent on some overhang of limestone,
the earth's floor thousands of feet below,
the light a startling grey,
with not even the snatched cry of a starling
to oppose the silence –
a breath
that the other has rescinded,
will be taken, held
held until the blood sings out, cries
that the heart has swollen
and is hurting, trapped behind the ribs,
beating furiously –
and finally, innately, released.

II

Adjournment then,
between here and not –
time enough to shape
some small shining thing, pliable
as a burnished want; something
warm – perhaps with feathers,
pica jade or greyback pewter;

small formed, a talisman
of blunted swell and rise,
etched runes visible
bound in skin the colour of rain.
This could be ours, our time
forged in metal, a curio for all
the life we never shared.
I offer you this seedling,
this oval amulet, take it:
In some other time,
we'll use the breaths annulled
to coax life.

Dorothy Brophy

A Lasting Encounter

From a very young age, books have always been in my life, they have always been my favourite gift. However, I had never met a writer until I met Philip Casey in the summer of 1981 when I was 22 years old. I had just finished my first academic year teaching in Loreto Abbey Secondary School and naturally I thought I was grown-up and mature!

I was awestruck by the poet and the circle of creative people I met in his company in that brief meeting, which to the best of my recollection was at the railway station in Gorey as he was saying farewell to photographer and writer Marc Perez and his wife Brigitte. I was returning to my family home in Dublin after a few days at the Gorey Arts Festival. This was my first experience of an arts festival, and I was thrilled by it all.

Marc, Brigitte and I sat together on the train. The chat was mostly about writing, and especially about Philip's writing. Philip's first collection of poems had been published in 1980, so Brigitte wrote the title down for me. Foolishly I tried every bookshop in Dublin looking for a copy of *Close Distant Summers* until finally in Parsons on Baggot Street Bridge, one of the wise proprietors corrected me and produced a copy of *Those Distant Summers*, which I still have today.

Details of our next encounter are at this remove unclear to me, though it may have been because I was teaching Philip's beloved sister Karina, and in the summer of 1985 we reconnected. I think it was probably at the wedding of Anita Webb and Tim Ball in St Michael's Church, Gorey, which was incidentally one of the most special weddings I have ever attended.

As I recall, between the main reception at Kia-Ora Farm Guesthouse and the evening event held at the Railway

Hotel in Gorey, we walked the beach in Ballymoney hand in hand before joining the evening party in town. We spent a lot of time together that summer and early autumn. A key memory is that we travelled to the Beara peninsula in West Cork (where I have lived since I left Gorey in 1989) to visit his Mum's sister Gertie and her husband John who was a native of Bere Island. Philip had never been to Beara before, and I was only too delighted for the excuse to visit Castletownbere, my mother's homeplace. I drove him all around the peninsula and brought him on the ferry to Bere Island. A particular memory is while standing behind me in Cahirkeem, a very beautiful spot on the north side of the Beara peninsula, looking across to Gortahig, Kenmare Bay and the Skelligs, Philip spotted a grey hair on the back of my head. I was only twenty-six and initially horrified. However, it very quickly became a joke and I think part of me felt it was a sign of maturity ... if only that's all it took!

I fell a little in love with Philip but I think I also felt out of my depth to some degree and so sadly I let him go. However, he has always held a special place in my heart and, some months before he died, we had a brief conciliatory conversation. Looking back now I can see what drew us together, our mutual interests such as literature and music and of course Gorey. There was also a shared experience of serious health issues and crises. In Philip's case his own health, in mine it was the health issues and crises of my father and brother, both of whom are also sadly long dead. There was a sharing of experience and trauma which was very comforting to me. My brother met him once and I remember hearing the pair of them howling with laughter in the kitchen while I was upstairs gathering my luggage to return to Gorey.

In the intervening years, I followed Philip's career and read most of what he had published and often heard news of him through friends in Gorey. I was blessed to have spent special time with him at a key time in my life, and I regard our shared time as a unique gift. Through my work in Cork County Library Service where I have worked since 1995 and my involvement in various arts festival events in Beara, I have met many writers, but none can match the magic and inspiration of being a friend of Philip's, albeit for a relatively short while, a long time ago.

We don't meet people by accident. Everyone is meant to cross our path for a reason.

Frank Callery

THE FABULIST
i.m. Philip Casey, February 4th, 2018

In the nonesuch of market banter
You will be dressed
As you swing through the gait
Of your everyday.
Anna calls from the quay
Liffey-shift to the cochlea's slush
A tinnitus of triads and hurt trochees.

You are beyond, hearing the gulls
In Fisher's and Boot, the clogged
Arteries of lost geographies
Whose echoes you negotiate
Deftly, in a trice, with rubber-touch –
The interstices of cobbles
That hinder with new rain.

The ABC of Abbey, of Synagogue,
Of Meetinghouse soon outstripped
As you turn for the Credit Union
Between the Boar's Head
And The Spice of Life.
You will rest and bring to account the found nuggets
Your pen turned in the glistening furrow.

Fabulist of hurt days, of hungered love;
Who will dress the streets with Maybloom now?
Who will regale them with tales of Al-Andalus?
Who will sing the song they are shorn of?
They will miss your wand, your arias.
The westering light will bring them shadows
And Arran Street will sulk in the silence.

Siobhan Campbell

GRAPE PICKING
for Philip Casey

There's a dark heavy smell under the vines
Where we move on our knees, bunch by bunch.
Secateurs cutting, bucket receiving grapes,
The air here fills with the fall of their weight.

The drop of skin onto skin is a spell –
A sound of warmth in the rendered world.
Clouded with damp, these ripening fruit
Purple our cramped space with ambivalence.

Hope lives, we learn, the right side of mould.
Too much heat now and all is lost.
We plan to go to the pressing to watch
The next stage in their long move.

Despite keeping no god, it could be a prayer
That passes between us as we clear the vines,
Not a sign of something but a kind of song
Sung to our settled selves.

That we each feel it, crawling and stretching,
Cutting receiving, shins flattened, backs cracked,
Even the fittest amongst us suffering; this, and
The sense of it all continuing keeps us going.

The trick would be how to hold this thing,
How to take it away on trains and boats
Hitching back to the cities, the college
Dorms or the stifling homes.

By the last day, we know it is gone
As soon as we're up in the cart; the late start,
The cleared scarp; only a few vines
To be done and they are the bitter fruit,

Left just too long, better for raisin,
Maybe for rum, not for wine,
The sweet, bevelled wine that from
Now on we will drink to high heaven.

Moya Cannon

THE HIGHEST HOUSE

His mother came, he said,
from halfway up a valley in Fanad.
Theirs was the last house in the valley,
she'd said, where the children weren't hired
to a farmer in Tyrone or the Lagan.

Once, further west, I drove three miles
up a bog road, in the dark, to a house so high
it was named for the crag-roosting king of birds.
A small, lit-up hostel under the hilltop, it rocked
with young life – hikers, holiday-makers,
from Japan, Germany, Holland.

The cottage had been bought, extended,
after the death of an old, cranky man,
who was hired at the fair,
for six months at the age of six,
instead of at the usual nine or ten.
The boy's sister, said the hostel owner,
was hired out at the age of seven,
"No one," he said, shaking his head
"was that poor."

What did he,
what do we, know now
of the humiliations
of hunger and servitude,
of having your arm-muscles felt
at a hiring-fare,
of the toss-penny chance
of landing in a good place
or a bad one,

of the slow burn
of anger
down the generations?

Young Philip

John Casey

GOD BETWEEN US AND SMALL FARMS

Philip Casey was born on 27 June 1950 in 42 Citizen Road, Hackney, London to our Irish emigrant parents, Pat and Anne Casey. The family later moved to 48 Wedmore Street in Islington where Peter and I, his two younger brothers, were born. This was to become our permanent London family home.

At the age of two, Philip developed a malignant cancerous tumour in his groin – devastating news for our parents. He underwent pioneering radium treatment in London's Royal Northern Hospital over a number of anxious months. The cancer eventually disappeared but the aggressive treatment involved was to have repercussions for him later in life.

Philip was taught by nuns in his first school in Islington. He was a most inquisitive little boy and would occasionally go missing. He'd often lift the latch on the front door of the family home and go wandering around the streets, even amongst the post-war bombsites. He'd always make it back home though, often in a Black Mariah, a London police van for transporting prisoners. It could be said therefore that this little kid was known to the police.

In 1957, our parents moved the family back to Ireland, having bought a small farm near Screen village in County Wexford, a place called Ballintaggart. We were to live here for three years. Philip, Peter and I attended Screen National School. Being slapped with a leather for spelling mistakes and being teased in the schoolyard on account of his Cockney accent came as a shock for Philip, but he adapted well and made many friends.

Life at home on the farm in Ballintaggart was a more exciting place than school for young Philip. After a

53

childhood spent living in a flat in the great city of London, this new life on a farm in Ireland was full of wonder for all three of us boys. Suddenly there was this newfound freedom in these amazing surroundings, so much space, so many things to investigate and explore. Philip learned quickly how to ride a bicycle and climbing trees became his specialty. An abiding memory is of him climbing to the pinnacle of one of our tall Macrocarpa trees, one hand grasping the uppermost branch, the other waving down at his panic-stricken mother.

But our family had to learn to work hard too and to pick up the vital skills of farm life such as how to milk cows and feed pigs. Sometimes even greater tasks had to be undertaken and Philip, being the eldest child, was often given difficult jobs to do. I can still see my nine-year-old brother heading off on his own with our donkey and cart to Ballyconniger mill three miles away with two bags of grain to be ground there, with part of his journey along the main road to Wexford town.

In the summer of 1961 we sold Ballintaggart and bought another house and farm in north County Wexford, Grove Mill, close to the village of Hollyfort. It was in an idyllic setting with the Bann River bordering its fields and the majestic Annagh Hill and Croghan Mountain keeping watch from a distance. This was to be the family home for the next thirteen years, the place where we were substantially reared, the place that to Philip was always home.

Philip, Peter and I were enrolled in Monaseed National School in September that year. By this time he was wearing a surgical boot as one of his legs was growing at a faster rate than the other. However, that didn't deter him from enthusiastically taking part in all school activities and giving his all. From the Myles Byrne Memorial Hall stage to the hurling and football field, Philip made his mark; likewise in athletics, outperforming others in the high jump and pole vaulting competitions in Gorey's Showgrounds. That was 1963. It was Philip's teacher in Monaseed, school principal Chris Clancy, who noticed his flair for writing in English, and encouraged it.

By now Philip was writing poems (or doggerel as he later referred to them). We'd come across verses scribbled on discarded pieces of paper, used school copybooks, wallpaper remnants, our father's discarded cigarette packets, anything he could write on. He took to writing songs too, boldly submitting a couple of them to Pye Records with the aid of his teenage friend and neighbour Pat Mordaunt, the proud owner of a tape recorder. He even posted an entry to the National Song Contest with the Eurovision in mind. No luck there unfortunately.

Life in Grove Mill in the early 1960s revolved around farmwork which was as relentless as it was tough: milking cows by hand twice a day, saving hay and cereal crops, thinning turnips. Philip thinned acres of turnips in his time; gruelling back-breaking and wrist-cramping work. But his response to the drudgery of it all would be to come out with a witty line or comment that would diffuse our resentment at having to work so hard. *God between us and small farms* was one of his many gems.

It wasn't all work and no play though. On summer evenings we would go hurling in our field by the bridge, a sport he loved. He was a fan of boxing as well. Inspired by the exploits of Cassius Clay/Muhammad Ali in the early 1960s he and his friend Pat set up a boxing ring in a field by the river, hazel rods for the corner posts, binding twine for the ropes. Neighbouring lads joined in and they'd spar for hours, Philip giving as good as he got. He'd regularly visit his neighbours, especially War of Independence veteran John Purcell with his troublesome leg and Mr and Mrs Tomkins, the old couple who lived in a tiny house by the river. He'd spend endless hours chatting with them.

In October 1964 Philip's schooldays in Monaseed National School were brought to an abrupt end when he was admitted into Cappagh Orthopaedic Hospital in Dublin to undergo life-changing surgery. By this time his left leg had grown five and a half inches longer than his right leg. To rectify this, surgeons in Cappagh were going to stop the growth of this 'good leg' and by putting tractions on the slower-growing leg they were to equalise their length.

In all, he was to spend almost three and a half gruelling years in that hospital undergoing countless painful procedures – and suffering painful aftereffects. In typical fashion though, he shielded us from anything that might worry us. In his many letters home he depicted Cappagh Hospital as paradise on earth. The nurses were pretty and friendly, and celebrities visited regularly to entertain. They even had their own school and a famous author named Eoghan Ó Tuairisc was teaching them English. Philip won a prize for the best essay on the poet Keats, a ten bob note out of the teacher's own pocket – no mean feat. Best of all was the number of friends he made there, especially a young fellow named Paddy Doyle who taught him how to play the guitar. He was also from Wexford. They were to become lifelong friends.

On a couple of rare visits home, however, it became obvious to us that all wasn't as promising as he was leading us to believe. He couldn't hide it, as much as he tried. In bed at night he would wake up in agony, the sinews in his neck stretched to skin-bursting point as he'd cry out in pain with a tortured look on his face. I remember feeling scared. Our parents must have been beside themselves with worry. They were solving his main problem as they saw it in Cappagh but this was coming at a hefty price.

Philip arrived home to Grove Mill from Cappagh by ambulance in June 1967, bag in one hand, guitar in the other, two feet firmly on the ground. He was fixed and finished with Cappagh forever – or so it was thought.

Three months later, Philip, now aged 17, started secondary school in Gorey CBS as a second-year student. The Christian Brothers kindly bent the rules to allow this. Although missing out entirely on First Year he fitted in well and made friends easily. He coped well with his subjects too, with the exception of maths which he just couldn't get to grips with. In his first Christmas algebra exam, he was unable to attempt even one question. Not willing to hand up an empty page however, he penned a short poem for his teacher Tom Flaherty. The first two lines went as follows:

X I never understood
Y I do not know

Tom certainly didn't see that coming but he enjoyed the poem immensely. Though not a teacher of English he was an English literature enthusiast and shared his passion for books with many of his students. He was to become an admirer of young Mr Casey (as he called him) and gave him every encouragement.

Someone else who greatly influenced Philip while in secondary school was classmate Aidan Breen, child genius, the boy who gave a lecture on quantum physics while in primary school. They became good friends and had a lot in common. They were both widely read and shared a wide range of intellectual interests. They regularly visited each other, exchanging books and ideas. Aidan would go on to become a renowned medievalist and scholar before his untimely death.

Other than a set of encyclopedias that our parents purchased to further our secondary school education, books weren't a prominent feature in our house in Grove Mill. That said, our mother occasionally picked up a book or two in Gorey for Philip to satisfy his voracious appetite for reading – and they weren't Mills and Boon. It was some time in the summer of 1968, when Philip was recovering from a ferocious kick from a cow, when she arrived home with a major present for him, a huge black-covered paperback with gold print on the cover, *Ulysses*, by James Joyce. He got stuck into it immediately and read it by daylight and by candlelight until he had finished it. Then he launched into *Moby Dick*, another whopper of a book she had found for him somewhere.

Philip was twenty-one-years-old when he sat his Leaving Certificate in Gorey CBS, his final year (1970–71) interrupted by another long stint in Cappagh hospital. Going on to university was an option but that didn't interest him. Almost immediately he started a course in typing and shorthand in Gorey Technical School under the watchful eye of teacher Mrs Donnellan. Each day he'd cycle in from Hollyfort on our mother's bicycle for those vital crash-course lessons. It was his idea.

It was around this time that Philip began writing poetry in a serious way and involved himself in the fledgling Funge Arts Centre in Gorey, the first of its kind anywhere in the country. Well-known local poet James Liddy had heard about his poetry writing and asked him to contribute to a poetry broadsheet he was publishing to coincide with the opening of the festival. After that he was to become a regular contributor to the festival literary magazine, *The Gorey Detail,* along with other writers such as Michael Considine, Eamonn Wall, Dermot Healy, Colm Tóibín and Francis Stuart. He was to remain a loyal supporter of the Gorey Arts Festival (as it was later called) in the years that followed.

By late 1971 Philip had moved to Dublin. His first permanent residence was a bedsit in 46 Beechwood Avenue in Ranelagh where he shared a house with his old pal from Cappagh, Paddy Doyle and a group of Paddy's friends. This was a most happy time in his life, a whole new world with friends calling, records playing, parties that went on long into the night. He worked in a number of jobs in the city, in Noyeks hardware shop in Camden Street, as an assistant to philatelist David Feldman in Harold's Cross, and in a cancer research laboratory, the Medical Research Council, in Trinity College.

It was around this time that our sister Karina was born in Wexford, the first baby to be brought up in Grove Mill for generations. A strong lifelong bond was to develop between them.

By 1974, while still working in Trinity, Philip had moved to a flat in Harcourt Terrace. After leaving work in Trinity on the evening of 17 May 1974, he narrowly missed being a victim of the Dublin bombings atrocity. As he stopped to chat with a work colleague for a few minutes in Westland Row, the devastating bomb went off around the corner in South Leinster Street. His journey home each day was always through South Leinster Street. Some angel was watching over him that evening. His poem, 'Those Distant Summers', echoes this terrible event.

In the summer of 1975 Philip and his close friend Tony Corbett (former flatmate in Beechwood Avenue) left Ireland and moved to Barcelona to teach English there. He quickly got a job teaching English to the family of a distinguished doctor, Señor Manchon. This he did for three years, developing an affectionate relationship with the Manchon family. They even came over to Ireland years later to visit him.

Spain was still a dictatorship when Philip lived there. In letters home, he described the fear and the repression that opponents of the Franco regime suffered at the time. He was also there when Franco died in 1977 and described the joy and elation in the streets on the announcement of his death. In Philip's words: *There wasn't a bottle of champagne to be had anywhere in the country such were the celebrations.*

More than likely he was out amongst the revellers in Placa Lesseps that night, his stomping ground in Barcelona.

Having lived in Spain for three years, Philip had acquired a good grasp of the Spanish language which enabled him to read Spanish literature and Spanish poetry in particular. He adored the poems of Federico García Lorca and translated some of them into English. (In Blanchardstown hospice, weeks before his death, he was happily translating a poem in Spanish for Ronan's Sheehan's anthology of *Cuban Love Songs*).

While on the continent he took the opportunity to go grape picking with friends in the Marne Valley in France in the autumn of '76 and '77. He returned to Ireland in late '77 and then headed back to France for another season of grape picking in '79. Four years later he was to travel to Israel, visiting such places as Bethlehem, the West Bank, the Negev Desert, and the Red Sea. Wherever he went in the world though he'd always make it back to Gorey for the Arts Festival as he was deeply involved in all the activities there.

It was during these years, in particular during the late 1970s and early 1980s, that he began to devote his entire life to creative writing. Annaghmakerrig, the artists' retreat in County Monaghan, was where he would escape to time and time again to write in solitude.

Between 1979 and 1986 Philip rented a basement flat in Longwood Avenue off the South Circular Road in Dublin, his first permanent residence after returning from Spain. He struck up a convivial relationship with his landlord, Mr Coughlan who lived upstairs, a friendly and jovial character with a fascinating life's story – which Philip recorded for posterity.

By 1983 he had developed severe circulation problems in his right leg, the leg with such a troubled history. An amputation below the knee was carried out in the Mater Hospital. A severe infection that he picked up after his amputation kept him in that hospital for almost a year – a year of severe pain and misery. *What age are you now Philip?* a hospital doctor asked him one day. *Thirty three,* answered Philip ruefully, *the same age as Christ crucified.*

After recuperating at home in Wexford for a number of weeks following his surgery, Philip returned to Longwood Avenue where he resumed his writing and his Dublin life. Though plagued by severe phantom pain, much of his finest poetry was written in this period.

In 1987 Philip moved to an apartment on Inchicore Road, close to Kilmainham Jail where he lived for over a year, a rich period of social and artistic engagement for him. In July 1988 he moved into his own house, just off Ormond Quay, 56 Arran Street East. Then in 1989 he was accepted as a member of Aosdána. His literary creativity went into overdrive after that and a period of intense productivity followed.

Unfortunately for Philip, life was to take another cruel twist in the early 1990s. He was in constant pain and try as he might, he couldn't mask it at times. His partial amputation in 1983 hadn't solved his circulation problem. Then in 1993, the inevitable happened. The remainder of his right leg would have to go, all of it. This was a cruel setback but one he faced with typical stoicism and wit. He requested a local anaesthetic. As the Mater Hospital surgeons were about to do the deed, a nurse, handing him earphones, asked him, *Philip, what music would you like to listen to? Oh, anything by The Saw Doctors!* he smiled. In his recovery ward, a kind and well-intentioned nun tried her best to console him. *Philip,* she said, *you're suffering for the sins of the world ... No sister,* replied Philip, *I'm suffering for the sins I'm going to commit as soon as I get out of here!*

Philip wore a prosthesis on his lower leg after his first amputation in 1983. Now he had to wear a full artificial leg which caused him severe discomfort and pain. He tried out several substitute prostheses but to no avail. He ditched them, opting for a set of crutches instead. They were to accompany him everywhere from then on, to poetry readings, book launches, lectures, marches (for causes close to his heart), and overseas. His outdoor schedule was busy at times as he always made himself available to support family, friends, fellow writers and artists.

In June 1996 Philip was amongst a group of Irish poets who were invited to Sicily to showcase Ireland's modern poetry, an initiative of the Italian Cultural Institute in conjunction with Poetry Ireland. It was an enormously successful visit with enjoyable and well-attended poetry readings in Catania University and in various mountain villages. Towards the end of the visit however, one of the younger Irish poets, Joe Woods, almost drowned while taking a swim in the sea near a Sicilian poet's summerhouse, a traumatic experience for his Irish and Italian companions. As his exhausted and panic-stricken rescuers delivered their unconscious friend onto the rocks, Philip lowered his crutches down the slope for them to grab onto, losing one of them into the choppy sea. Mercifully Joe was revived in hospital and desperation turned to relief – and Philip's crutches were replaced by the same hospital.

56 Arran Street East, with its distinctive red door, original sash windows and colourful front garden was to be a most creative and welcoming place, a sanctuary for friends from all over the world. All who called there were greeted with open arms and a strong warm handshake. He had good times with his neighbours on Arran Street as well, and had great affection for them. They had great affection for him also.

Yes, Philip thrived in good company and loved to regale his audience with a good story, with laughter and song. While alone however, his house was his workplace and he toiled there in solitude, and though often in excruciating pain, he was focused on his work, cutting out obvious distractions such as television and radio.

Aided and abetted by his computer genius godson Shane Doyle, Philip became a technological wizard, an early user of the internet and a self-taught web designer, designing sites for many of his friends. His own website *philipcasey.ie* charted his own literary career while his *irishwritersonline* was a vast and much-used resource for anyone interested in biographical information on Irish writers. Some of his time was spent answering correspondence generated by this site. He was a respected literary critic and reviewed poetry at different times for the *Sunday Tribune*, the *Sunday Independent* and the *Sunday Press*.

After he had finished his three novels, the Bann River Trilogy, Philip's final project was a daunting one, a history of the Irish race, from the first peoples who migrated to Ireland up to modern times. What started out as a history of Ireland's involvement in the slave trade developed into something far more challenging and ambitious. It consumed him for twelve years, possibly longer than that.

Slavery and Ireland's involvement in the slave trade in the Caribbean in the wake of the Cromwellian plantation was the main theme in Philip's novel, *The Fisher Child* (2001) and the subject of a number of his talks and lectures on this dark side of Irish history. He read from *The Fisher Child* at the International Conference of the Spanish Association for Irish Studies in Tenerife in 2010. Two Brazilian academics were duly impressed and put his book on their Irish Studies and Caribbean Studies courses. They later invited him to Brazil to speak to students at the South American Association for Irish Studies in São Paulo in 2011. This was a great honour.

Another great honour for him was the 'Evening for Philip' in 2015 in Dublin's Mansion House, organised by his good friends and fellow writers Katie Donovan and

Dermot Bolger. This was to celebrate his 65th birthday and the publication of his collection of poems, *Tried and Sentenced: Selected Poems,* compiled and edited by his close friend Marion Kelly. Predictably a large crowd of fellow writers, family, friends and admirers were there to express their love and admiration for him. Some of us read from his work, while Philip listened, modestly enjoying the attention.

That Mansion House celebration was a timely one as Philip's general health had begun to deteriorate visibly by then. Those of us close to him could see it in his eyes. Yet nothing could take him away from his magnum opus, his history of Ireland, plus a whole range of other projects and undertakings. Deep down he knew he was in trouble. He'd never complain though and would make light of his suffering. *How are you today Philip?* he'd be asked. *Agh,* he'd say, *if I was a horse I'd be shot.*

Philip died in St Francis's Hospice in Blanchardstown in Dublin on 4 February 2018. One of the finest human beings on this earth was gone. We will never see the likes of my brother again.

The Casey brothers

50th birthday: Mary Manley (married to Michael Considine), Aileen Casey (married to Peter Casey), Geraldine Byrne (RIP, married to John Casey)

Stephen Considine (Philip's godson), Karina Casey, Vincent Casey (Philip's nephew) and Eadaoin Casey (Philip's niece)

Karina Casey

UTTERLY PHILIP

When I was asked to contribute to this anthology, a question kept popping into my mind. Where do I start? How do I begin to convey what a kind, empathetic, strong person he was? I need him here to guide me as that is exactly what Philip did from the day I was born. He guided, encouraged and protected me.

Philip was 21 when I burst into my parents' and three brothers' lives. To say I was a surprise was an understatement, at least that was what my mother always said. Some of my favourite photographs of Philip and I were taken when I was a baby, as he gently cradled me in his arms. We became the best of friends instantly and I followed him everywhere. He never minded me cramping his style and he always proudly introduced me to his friends. I felt on top of the world. He would patiently listen to my little stories as if they were great works of literature. I adored him and he adored me. On my 15th birthday Philip wrote me a beautiful letter in which he told me how much I meant to him and all the family and that if the next few years were trying and difficult, I was to remember that I was loved and that he would always be there. I told him a few years before he died how much that letter meant to me and that I still had it. He was very moved and hugged me. Philip was the world's best hugger; no matter where or when we met I always got a hug and it made the world seem a brighter, safer place.

Philip was in hospital many times before and after I was born. There were three standout stays that are forged into my mind. When I was 12, Philip was in the Mater for a long period of time. On one occasion Mam and Dad returned from visiting Philip and they broke the news to me that Philip had an amputation. He came home to Gorey after his stay in hospital to recover and our bond grew stronger.

In 1988 our parents decided to move closer to the family in Dublin and Philip moved into his new home. I remember the night he rang Mam and Dad and told them he saw a house in the city centre. He was so excited. My parents and I were in Dublin to see the house the following weekend and I remember a look that passed between Philip and our father that went beyond words, and my mother nodding in agreement. It was perfect.

In the early 1990s Philip was in hospital for a long period of time again; another amputation. At that stage I was working in the city centre and I would pop up to see him in the hospital at lunchtime or in the evening after work. He was writing *The Fabulists* at the time. He would write pages during the week in hospital and give them to me to type and bring back to him. I think that is why *The Fabulists* is my favourite of all of Philip's books. I got to know Mungo and Tess before anyone else. I was always in awe of how he could portray a simple event with such eloquence and beauty. Since Philip died I found great comfort in his poetry, in particular *Dialogue in Fading Light*, which includes 'Utterly You' which was one of the poems Philip dedicated to me.

We were great pals and we went on many adventures together, including a visit to Boston and New York. One of the highlights of the trip was a visit to MIT in Boston. He was fascinated. He was ahead of his time, and I think there were a lot of inventions in his mind yearning to escape. I remember a particularly turbulent flight from Boston to New York in a small plane. Philip held my hand during the flight to keep me calm and once we landed in New York he burst out laughing. He never knew I was so strong. His hand was still white from my crushing it during the flight. I told him it was in our DNA, and he laughed heartily again. His strength and determination were immeasurable. He was so courageous, often chatting away to someone without them knowing what a struggle he was going through. I got to know the signs and we kept it between ourselves.

Our father died in 2011 at home surrounded by the family, and in 2014 our mother died peacefully in hospital. Philip and I were on either side of her bed. Again, Philip was my protector and he guided me through this painful time, even though he was trying to navigate his way through the mourning process himself.

In January 2017 Philip was admitted to hospital. He tried to protect me once again. He tried to protect everyone. He didn't want anyone to worry. He always got through these obstacles in the past, but sadly it was different this time. He got home before Christmas and he was so excited to spend Christmas with me in my new home. We rarely missed a Christmas together but this was to be our last one.

Philip brightened the lives of everyone he met. I loved meeting him unexpectedly walking through the city. How he managed his crutches on the cobblestones of Temple Bar remains a mystery. He is never far from my thoughts. He was my brother and also my Godfather. His kindness, patience and wisdom have guided and given me strength through the last few years without him. I think of Philip throughout each day, and sometimes unknowingly a single tear falls on my cheek and it reminds me how grateful I am for having Philip in my life.

Philip Casey

UTTERLY YOU

I can see you as utterly you.
Your laugh is unlike the music

of angels, or the first young thrush
of the day – it's simply your laugh,
fresh to the earth, and beautifully
free of simile. Look at me now.
Your eyes are not pools of light,
but guileless, flesh and blood eyes
that can break my heart with delight.
I've never seen twin silver streams
glisten on your pale alabaster cheeks –
only ever salt tears, like those
I remember crying before my heart
grew calm and learned to listen.

Philip and his brother John, with Paul Kavanagh, Gorey CBS, 1969

Philip with his parents after The Fabulists *book launch*

Philip with his beloved sister, Karina

Peter Casey

MEMORIES OF BIG BROTHER, PHILIP

The realisation that Philip looked out for his baby brother (me) and still does, has become stronger recently. He understood and supported my fascination with tropical islands, swaying palms and echoey shimmering strings. The first book I read was back in the sixties. It was entitled *On Copra Ships and Coral Isles*, which Phil rooted out for me in the old Gorey Library. He continued to keep an eye out for anything relating to Hawaii or the South Pacific, such as books, magazines, TV documentaries and guitar music. The personal memories that follow contain little of his writings but illuminate events that may have shaped them. However, this collection of random recollections would not be complete without briefly referring to my favourite poem of his. Its evocative title triggers something deep in me. In Philip's final hours, in the muted light of the hospice room, I tried to read aloud 'Those Distant Summers' but after the second verse, I had to be rescued by my wife, Aileen and my sister-in-law, Geraldine, RIP.

The Casey boys, of Wexford, Philip, John, and Peter, were born in London, in the 1950s. Our sister, Karina, is the only family member to be born under the Purple and Gold in the 1970s. *Why Wexford?* was a question that my father was asked. *That's where the boat docked* was his practiced retort whenever this query arose. After a short dalliance near Screen, we settled in Hollyfort and haven't really left there since. To be exact, Dad bought a small farm called Grove Mill down the hill from Hollyfort village. This old house with its energy, history and strange sounds in the night, was set in a veritable botanical garden with many flower, shrub and tree varieties we hadn't seen before. One side of the farm has the Bann River as a natural boundary. There are wooded areas, a millrace full of eels, a secret field and many other quirky features. So much wonderment to fuel the imagination of a boy who had played with discarded gas masks in the bomb sites of London a few years previously. In the early days, neighbours would drop by to introduce themselves and fill us in on the latest gossip. They quickly recognised Phil's interest in local historical figures such as the infamous Hunter Gowan, Father Sweetman, who grew tobacco commercially in the 1940s, and many colourful neighbourhood characters.

One day Mum arrived home from Gorey with a purple-handled penknife that Phil had requested. She enquired with mock fear, *What do you need it for? You'll see*, he replied, while heading towards the turnip shed where we kept winter feed for the cows. I recall Dad opening the shed door that evening and saying *Oh fuck* as forty strange turnip heads stared back at him. Our cows didn't appreciate Phil's sculpting talents as they munched on his Easter Island-like culinary art.

It wasn't unusual for Phil to take his guitar off to one of the fields, with Croghan, his magical inspirational mountain in the distance, to write songs. 'On the Road to Carney' was one of his compositions penned during the ballad boom of the late 1960s. A tale of a young lad missing his dead mother. Its only public performance was in the Kilmuckridge folk and ballad song contest in 1971. As John was in college, this was my chance to sing in public with Phil. John and Phil had quite a repertoire of songs by The Bachelors and Jim Reeves, which they performed for neighbours and won local talent contests. Thankfully an internet search doesn't reveal any information about this song contest; the people of Kilmuckridge have suffered enough.

Philip was a gentle giant and very forgiving of people's indiscretions, with one exception, those who discard cellophane cigarette wrappers on the footpath. These invisible booby traps are not crutch friendly and caused him many a tumble and skinned nose.

One of Phil's classmates recently confided in me that when the Caseys first attended Monaseed school, a gang of boys would frequently pick on Philip and jump on top of him like a rugby tackle. At that time, Phil had a lift on his shoe and probably had a hint of a London accent. My informant added that he has always felt bad about not intervening. However, Phil quickly became popular in school and reversed that situation which had the potential to turn nasty.

His favourite hurling position was in goal, as his disability limited his mobility. When his shovel-like hands went up to catch a speeding sliotar, bodies were sent flying in all directions as he charged forward to clear the goal line. His upper body strength was phenomenal and his handshake memorable. A handshake with Philip Casey was like a handshake from a JCB. He won popularity through his musical comedy performances at school concerts in the local Myles Byrne Memorial Hall. Songs such as 'The Bold Thady Quill' about a Cork hurling legend and 'Are you there Moriarity' a tale of a jovial Dublin policeman, were acted out with exaggerated gyrations as he worked the audience into hysterical laughter. It soon became known that Phil had a talent for writing and storytelling. He would often discreetly help classmates with spellings and ideas for essays. My brother John clearly remembers Philip being repeatedly prodded in the ribs with a pen by a chap vehemently pleading *Givis a sentence, Casey*. When no response was forthcoming, a threat was issued *Givis a sentence, Casey, or I'll stick this fucking pen up your arse*. I have since wondered if that chap unwittingly inspired the title of Philip's last publication, *Tried and Sentenced*.

In April 1967 an Irish horse called 'Foinavon', a complete outsider, won the Aintree Grand National. At breakfast that Saturday morning an argument over toast occurred between Phil and Dad. I still recall Dad roaring, *who do you think you are?* to which Phil replied with equal volume, thumbing his own chest to emphasise each word, *I'm me.* The shouting got louder as the row moved upstairs, amplified by the empty bedrooms. Both returned red-faced to the kitchen a while later, where we all continued breakfast in silence. Between Phil and Dad this silence continued for about six months, until one day when Dad was in Dublin on business, he called to Cappagh Hospital to see Phil. The only comment Dad made on his return was, *he can play the guitar, you know.* Being a gifted musician himself, Dad couldn't hide his pride. Phil's way of reflecting on the futility of such an event would be to say, *those men are sleeping now.*

Phil's partner in crime in Cappagh Hospital was Paddy Doyle who later wrote *The God Squad*, an account of his early life in an industrial school. In 1973 I became Paddy and Phil's housemate in Beechwood Avenue, Ranelagh where every Saturday night there was a party; Kristofferson, Buddy Holly or Cat Stevens on the record player, several guitars strumming along and Tony Corbett doing what is now called stand up. On one occasion the landlord, Big John, joined the party with cooked chickens, chips and large bottles of lemonade. With a grin he said, *Lads, I've had a complaint about the noise.* Big John produced a 'Baby Power' and joined in the singing. A knowing wink from Phil reassured me, the redneck rookie, that this was a regular act.

Aileen and I bought our house in Lucan in 1981. To say that money was tight is an understatement. Phil came to visit us one evening shortly after we had moved in, but we had gone shopping and in those pre-mobile phone days, we missed each other. However, he had dropped an envelope through the letterbox. I have heard from many sources since that this discreet white envelope act of generosity was his trademark. He is the Phil in philanthropy.

Once when I visited Phil in the hospice, we got nostalgic about guitars, music and songs. Somehow, 'The Liverpool Lullaby' came up in conversation and suddenly Phil commanded, *Sing it.* Without hesitation, I started singing at the top of my voice using the room echo to great effect, and the forgotten words came back to me. Not only that but it was tuneful, on key, and my self-consciousness, which had previously prevented me from singing in public, was gone. I was in an altered state, it was like magic, I could sing, it must have been the Phil factor.

At Philip's funeral several people recalled how his skills as a listener had helped them to get through some tough times. I knew exactly what they meant. Often when I had a difficult issue, I would visit Philip for a coffee. Floating away from Arran Street an hour later, my problems had evaporated. He was a natural therapist without realising it. One of Phil's female friends, who was a regular attendee at the Beechwood sessions, whispered in my ear as the crematorium curtains closed to the playing of 'The Parting Glass', *he was the glue that kept us together.*

Philip died on 4 February 2018, which is 'World Cancer Day'. In 1953, when he was three years of age, he was diagnosed with sarcoma of the groin, a bone and tissue cancer. At the time, the treatment for this diagnosis was to burn the cancer away with radium. In Phil's case, good tissue was destroyed resulting in one leg developing at a slower pace than the other. Then followed years of surgical shoes, leg lengthening traction which he said was like medieval torture, amputation after amputation and all accompanied by heavy-duty drugs to manage pain. Phil had a sense that he was being experimented on, like donating his body to medical science while he was still alive. Hopefully, some good has come from his lifetime of bravery and suffering.

In 2019, Aileen and I, helped by Tony Corbett, his partner Reyés and our cousin Kathy, scattered some of Philip's ashes under a tree in Parc de la Ciutadella, Barcelona's main public park. In the 1970s Phil and Tony had made a new life for themselves in the Born area of the city. They would often sit beneath these trees reading and soaking up the Catalan sun. Tony regaled us with memories of their escapades and pointed out many addresses where they had lived and some of their favourite bars and cafés. Philip's ashes are in several other locations including in Vigo, Spain, the foothills of Croghan, the Bann River and one of the fields in Grove Mill. His headstone is a blue plaque on the Bann River bridge in Hollyfort and his portrait by Eamonn Carter hangs in Gorey Library. I'm sure he would see the humour in the notion of being hanged in Gorey.

Whether swinging his imaginary hurl as Thady Quill, hacking through the frozen clay of potato pits in winter, stomping grapes in Champagne or picking strawberries in the sizzling Wexford sun, Philip lived every moment. I insisted that the breastplate of his coffin read; Philip Casey lived 1950–2018. Whenever I'm close to Arran Street, I recall the words of poet Frank Callery who captured Philip's essence in his tribute poem 'The Fabulist' – 'They will miss your wand, your arias and Arran Street will sulk in silence'. I sometimes take a saunter past Philip's red door, number 56, half expecting to see him there, looking back again and again before turning the corner, just in case he comes to the door. How privileged am I to have Philip as a big brother?

The last words I recall Philip saying are *I'm not afraid* and I believed him, strength of character to the end. Suzie Kennedy, the celebrant at Philip's funeral, used some words which I am borrowing to finish this glimpse into my memories of him. *I knew Philip, a little, back in the day.*

Philip with his niece Iseult for whom he wrote The Coupla

Patrick Chapman

THE WORLD IS WIDE:
PHILIP THE PIONEER

When I first met Philip Casey, sometime in the early 1990s, his poetry was already familiar to me. *The Year of the Knife* was magnificent, his voice as a poet unique. His previous collection, *After Thunder*, was an early influence. At that time, the internet was not in everyday use and the World Wide Web was just being born, so it was much later when Philip started to embrace the new technology. When it matured, he was ready for it.

Over the years we got to know each other a little. I remember coming over to his house for chats, not regularly but once in a while, and he'd always have good cheese and bread to share. His front room was one of those writerly spaces where a wall seemed made of books rather than bricks. I recall how generous Philip was with his enthusiasms. He seemed to have a notion of transcendence, of our place in the universe, but also a current, informed view on all kinds of issues. He had a zen-like unsentimental clarity of vision, and an openness to the new. I found him to be a gentle man whose core was powerful and strong.

As a writer, and especially as a poet, Philip was very much a pioneer in the field of technology and IT. He was way ahead of everyone, with his Irish Writers Online being a resource that took foresight and dedication. He was always aware of possibilities and quick to identify those with a future. As someone living with disability, he found it exciting to be able to take charge of things from home. He mentioned more than once how the internet was a game changer, liberating for everyone, not just him. Almost, you could say, a form of astral flight.

The first inkling I had that Philip was into this technology was when the Irish Writers Online website appeared in the late 1990s or early 2000s. He was an early adopter, collating and curating biographical information about Irish writers, creating a database that must have been immeasurably useful to academics and others who wished to get an encyclopaedic view of the subject. IWO featured not only current writers but potted biographies and bibliographies of Irish writers of the past. It preceded Wikipedia, and unlike many anthologies – though the IWO didn't showcase work – it was egalitarian. If you were a published Irish or Irish-based writer, you could send your details and Philip would post them. The curation here was light in that there seemed to be a house style simply for consistency and clarity.

IWO evolved with Philip's growing technological facility. He was a natural, developing his own website too, in one of the earliest examples of the kind for an Irish writer. He enjoyed learning from other writers around the world who also had websites. A particular favourite was BoingBoing, Cory Doctorow's site, which was ahead of the curve, and which Philip saw as a good source of discussion of future-adjacent areas such as socially conscious tech movements and electronic digital rights. Philip had a natural curiosity about how everything worked. So, he helped himself to become a digital citizen, and taught me a thing or two as well.

He had a rebellious attitude to the major corporations. Instead of running bespoke engines from Apple and Microsoft he preferred to work with open source software and independent platforms, such as Ubuntu, Creative Commons and WordPress. He liked their versatility, the fact that you could add your own stamp and weren't corralled within a walled garden. There was something of the frontier about the tech he favoured, and this suited his temperament. He once told me that the Web had given him a reach far greater than he might otherwise have expected – this, of course, being true of us all – and allowed his mind to wander all around the world, exploring, meeting new people, and exchanging ideas. It was an extension of his powers. Nowadays we all experience this online, and for most of us it's second nature. Twenty years ago, Philip was more advanced in his journey into cyberspace than many others. If there was a cutting edge, he turned it into skis.

Philip was very much an advocate for the internet in general. He saw it as a positive, empowering tool for anyone, anywhere, with access to it. Whether it was his experiences with traditional media, some of which were positive, some not so much, the idea of being able to make connections outside the confines of the old gatekeepers appealed to him. He saw the internet as a democratising tool, and a way for individuals to engage with each other politically as well as culturally. A medium is ethically and morally neutral and it's up to the user to bring their own. On balance, he saw the internet as a force for good.

During one of our occasional chats over cheese and coffee in his house – Philip had a fondness for the delicatessen from the Saturday market in Temple Bar – he brought up the idea of a new kind of website. It would be a place where authors could present their own out-of-print books and preserve them for posterity, or simply make them available again. This was 2006. During our chat, I thought of the phrase 'Irish Literary Revival', blurted it out, and Philip seized on it with alacrity. We had our idea. Determined to make it happen, I registered the URL and Philip built the site on WordPress. We contacted several authors, quite a few of whom were interested and sent us PDFs of their books for hosting. A designer friend of mine, Wendy Williams, volunteered a logo design, which used the letter 'i' in quotes so that it looked like an angel. The idea was to get the authors involved in preserving their work. We would have their permission to host it – unlike, say Google Books, who were hoovering up works left, right and centre. We distributed the books for free under a Creative Commons licence, with the consent of the writers. RTÉ even interviewed Philip and me on air about this new development.

Who did we have on our site? Sara Berkeley was a particular favourite, as back in the beginning of my writing career her extraordinary collection *Penn* had inspired me to try getting my own book published. Philip had other writers in mind, such as Terry McDonagh. As time went on it became clear that the site was no longer needed, as it was ever easier for writers themselves to host or republish their own out-of-print work.

The internet has changed so much since 2006, as we all know. Eventually, Philip decided to move on from the ILR, as he had his hands full with his other sites, as well as an enormous non-fiction book project he was working on, which I hope might yet see the light of day. He had also begun thinking about republishing his own novels and poetry. Throughout the run of the ILR project, I was struck by Philip's gentle encouragement, his enthusiasm, and his generosity in bringing back the books of other writers.

The Irish Literary Revival was not the last adventure Philip had online. As he told me, he'd long wanted to bring his first novel, *The Fabulists,* back into print. Originally published by Lilliput, a digital copy now resided on the ILR, as well as my own out-of-print debut, *Jazztown*. Philip had been delighted about having his next two novels, *The Water Star* and *The Fisher Child*, published by Picador, but they too seemed to be unavailable. Now that all three were out of circulation, he decided to bring them back via his own imprint, eMaker Editions, superseding the ILR as an example of how a single author could take control of their own publishing. I didn't work with Philip on eMaker, aside from happily being a sounding board for his cover design images. Along with the novels, he also put out a selection of his poetry, *Tried and Sentenced*. I proofed one version of this, but his great friend Marion Kelly of the *Parlour Review* edited the book, curating an essential and important selection of Philip's best poems. These new editions were made available as ebooks and in print-on-demand.

On my own shelves I have first-run print copies of his books, including *Those Distant Summers* – found via the internet – as well as hard copies of his new editions from eMaker. Original first printings of Philip's novels now go for the proverbial 'eye-watering prices' online, alongside the rather more accessible Kindle editions. His novel for children, *The Coupla*, is also available as an ebook.

When in 2013 the Canadian poet Dimitra Xidous, newly arrived in Ireland, approached me to set up an online poetry and art magazine, *The Pickled Body*, it felt in some small way a natural progression from my online collaboration with Philip. We were honoured to publish a poem of his; to me it felt like I had his blessing. *The Pickled Body* is currently on hiatus after nine issues and a joint exhibition with *Gorse* magazine at Maynooth University's art space. This brings to mind the subject of digital curation, a very different problem today from the challenges of 2006. In a world where ephemeral is the new normal, it might be desirable to create or revive an imprint to preserve Philip's work in one place for future generations and the interest of scholars.

Politically engaged, always welcoming, and one hell of a poet, Philip used the internet as a prism, refracting all the colours of life, in all kinds of directions. With a curiosity fed by a pure joy in discovering and adapting new technology, he used what he learned – and built – for the betterment of his fellow humans, as well as to keep alive words that otherwise might pass into history.

One of my final memories of seeing Philip is the celebration put on by his friends and colleagues at the Mansion House, Dublin, marking his sixty-fifth birthday. Dermot Bolger and Katie Donovan were the instigators of this, if I recall correctly. Ever humble, not fond of the limelight, Philip seemed genuinely moved by the whole experience. I hope that he truly understood how greatly he was loved and appreciated by those who gathered on that night to celebrate him and his work.

Every now and then, passing by on a tram, or crossing the river, I look down towards Arran Quay and expect to see Philip there. I imagine what it is like today, the house where Philip lived, its walls made of books, its kitchen full of welcome, its occupant a man who never complained about the hand he'd been dealt. His mind was a full house.

Jim Chapson

PHILIP

A long time ago (40 years?) when Philip was in a Dublin hospital recovering from one of his many surgeries, I thought to visit him, hoping to bring some cheer to his lonely day. Down a dismal corridor I heard voices; Philip's small room was crowded with friends. I pressed my way to the centre of the swirling chatter, where Philip lay propped up in bed, the stump of his amputated leg swathed in white bandages. He had been visited that morning, he told me, by a doctor who delivered an encomium on skin. Philip had found this very amusing; recounting the story he let loose his distinctive laugh: loud, resonant, and deep.

Christy Brown — art through the prism of lifelong illness

Christine Clear

Philip Dancing

Why can't I remember more? There were hundreds of nights spent with Philip in jovial, restless, intense, listless, fatigued company. I'd say, at the very least, we met once a month for 25 years. That's the guts of 300 nights. Somehow together or in company, early in the evening or late at night, in a restaurant or at home, we broke bread, and wine, or none or both. But now, strangely, I can't remember how Philip ate or drank. Other than having a 'fine' appetite I can't recall how he chewed his food or how he drank his wine or water, or beer or even his tea. I can still recall how he held his glass, his knife and fork, but I don't remember whether he was a noisy eater, necessarily slow or fast, if he chewed or just swallowed his food. I can't recall if he kept his mouth shut as he ate or sprayed the food across a table. I don't remember because most of our evenings were spent in some genre of conversation. Food was in general wholesome and, background. Of course, he was famous for his Rioja wine, his market cheeses and crackers, his dark chocolate and the many other culinary gifts. They fuelled the banter, the enraged insights, the volcanic laughter (Philip's), the trusted confessions, the absorbing history lessons.

Philip had so many lives, and I know his visits to us in Inchicore claimed only a tiny fraction of them. But for us *upriver*, they might have been all he'd ever known. What I'm saying is that Philip showed up. No matter his level of health, his presence was the foundation of each encounter.

It was the same if we were out and about at night. Over the years I was humbled by how many people softened in his company. How many shone and became effortlessly funny. How men suddenly became enlivened and jauntily attractive in a passing encounter, how women cracked jokes to him from across a room. He held a warm gravitas in a crowd. In smaller circles he held more. A deep civility. An older brother even amongst his elders, his humanity connected through his intelligence and learning. I witnessed so many hard-edged personalities listen to him speak, so many contrarians quell, mean drunks become avoidant. It was good fun being out with Philip because people around him behaved themselves. His lifetime sufferings I think garnered a kind of animal respect.

Philip was incredibly generous. I remember him being weighted by his endless coinage. A steel fixer was quieter on an empty street. He jingled as he limped, and I quipped how his loot created ballast for his undulating frame crossing on the Ha'penny Bridge. A running joke was that a chair fell backwards if Philip's coat was hung on it, and in all the years I've known Philip, he could draw up a bigger spill than anyone I knew. For sure, he moved through the city like a belled cat – a belled and beneficent cat. I don't think I ever saw him pass someone needing his spare money. This was his trust in life at play. Securing what he needed to create what was simple and comfortable, the rest was allowed to float. In fact, his generosity extended to everything. A clock never ticked with him, despite the time. No matter how tired or pained, he routinely attended Dublin's cultural events, his nightly to-ing and fro-ing from Arran Street humanising the quayside after dark. Although he occasionally slipped and fell on the foulest of streets, his resilience arose from that sometime humiliation and disgust.

Philip often worked deep into the night. It was his solitary kingdom. He loved his star beckoning skies and in the last years of his life, that kingdom colonised the mornings, and then plundered the early afternoons. In the end we knew better than to ring before it was tipping evening and the merriment from surrounding pubs thickened the soundscape of Arran Street East.

Philip's legacy for me as a writer, thinker, advocate, stems from his ability to celebrate life. He was an unblocked channel. I didn't appreciate it when he was alive, but I see now that he had a natural grace; he understood when to run and when to wait and his famous line, *The trick is to wait long enough*, is a flashing beacon which gets brighter each year. He knew life in ways I hope I never will, and he had a hugely energised relationship with his mind, his spirit, his soul. Like a dictator, a crusader, a gambler, an orphan (he said he was on the side of the defeated and the hopeless in his poem 'Symbol'), he knew how to live his life, how to trust it, love it. He picked his battles, he fought his justices. Turned his vulnerabilities to strengths. He wrote 4 novels and 5 collections of poetry. He had countless operations following a series of amputations. He held court in his house in Arran Street which expressed his genius for love and friendship. He over-laughed little jokes, confessed to profound loneliness, didn't quite get the nuances of toxic situations, was embittered with traditional Irish life.

But at the end of the day, when it came down to it – and when he put his mind to it – Philip. Could. Dance. He often confessed that he couldn't multitask – but in fact, he could. He could drink and, he could dance – I saw him at it many a time and oft, and, for the record, he was great craic on the dancefloor. So, my favourite memories abide of him with or without his crutches, shaking it to the gods with the best of them.

Wryly, Philip would confess to offering you his "pagan prayers" whenever they were asked for or needed. In fact, "Bless You!" became his signature sign-off on the phone, on his doorstep, getting into a taxi, on an email, a text, a tweet, as a salute. Everywhere, all the time, his blessing gathered his love into his encounters.

I know he felt blessed because he often said it, and somehow this prayer creeped into our everyday parlance and became so well established that no one could own it like him. In fact, if he had been buried and a headstone carved, I could think of no better epitaph. It was his quintessential and signature prayer. His will and wish for all things to live. We come from the stars, and to the stars we return, was another of his ditties, and for me, his grounding spirituality. This doesn't explain his exquisite humanity; the love he brought into the world, nor more importantly, the love he has left behind him in the world, but it does source his pedigree. He never left his doorstep before I turned the corner out of Arran Street. Always, there was a final wave. To his memory and to his everlasting legacy, this is my shared snapshot; Philip leaning over his green gate holding the street for you until you switched worlds. It was a blessing incarnate and everlasting and I recall it often to give me life.

Philip and Ulrike Boskamp on the Ha'penny Bridge

Kevin Connolly

THE WINDING STAIR

I opened The Winding Stair Bookshop and Café on Ormond Quay, Dublin in August 1982 in a small space on the first floor of a four-storey former textile factory. One day, shortly after opening, the poet Maurice Scully climbed the winding staircase that I shared with my then landlord, *In Dublin* magazine, and breathlessly asked me if I would consider allowing him and his fellow poets, Billy Mills and Randolph Healy, the opportunity to hold an 'event' in the shop. The first *Beau* event – the *Beau* being the eponymous literary magazine that they edited – took place a few weeks later and The Winding Stair as venue was born. It wasn't long before word got out among the alternative literary publishers that there was a new venue in town.

That's when I first met Dermot Bolger who was the driving force behind Raven Arts Press, the new kids on Ireland's poetry publishing block. Dermot attracted mainly younger writers to his imprint including the aforementioned Maurice Scully, Paul Durcan, Sara Berkeley, Pat McCabe, Conleth Ellis, Mathew Sweeney, Nuala Ní Dhomhnaill as well as more established writers such as Anthony Cronin, Michael Hartnett and Francis Stuart. Included in the Raven young poets 'stable' was a thirty-something Philip Casey. At one of the early Raven readings, I recall hearing Philip read. I can't remember the poem but I still recollect the way in which he mellifluously enunciated each precious syllable of his poem. Over the next two decades I came to know that voice and that sincerity, and that loyalty to the preciousness of the articulation of sound and language, and to the delicate breathtaking pellucid nature of his poetry.

Many will say how instantaneously friendships with Philip began. He was a kind and gentle man, possessing an intelligence and sense of humour that were both immediately recognisable and profound, and came with a light, delicate and, above all, respectfully mischievous touch. His own physical suffering had imbued him with a sense of empathy and compassion. The evening we first met I was on crutches resulting from a sports injury. I remember how, after the reading, we were making our way across the Ha'penny Bridge together heading for the International Bar for the traditional post-reading pints. Philip, also on crutches, raced over the steep incline of the bridge while I struggled to get up the steps. He came back to help, leaning on one crutch and extended his powerful free hand to drag me up, prompting me to ask how he had injured himself, assuming his was a sports injury like mine. He bent his head back and roared with laughter into the night. His crutches were a permanent requirement. He spent a lot of time in hospitals and indeed, one of his books of poetry, *The Year of the Knife*, reflects those times with penetrating, visceral observation. Yet I never heard him complain once about the undoubted pain he experienced on a daily basis. He just got on with things. That laugh became as familiar as the man himself.

Over the years I expanded the shop to embrace all four floors of that fine building, but The Winding Stair lost none of its intimacy. Philip became a permanent feature browsing among the shelves or sitting at the tables of the bookshop and café, particularly after he moved to his lovely terraced cottage in Arran Street East, a stone's throw from the shop. He brought his visitors there too and was often accompanied by a fellow poet, or by a procession of friends and admirers. All seemed as enthralled by Philip as we at The Winding Stair were.

During the 1990s and 2000s he attended and read at many of the scores of readings, music sessions, performances, exhibitions and lectures that were held at The Winding Stair, as well as the legendary parties that were staged in that beautiful rambling building on the quays. His humility was such that he imbued the works of other poets with the same degree of passion and intensity that he did his own. I recall one evening in particular when he and the poet Paula Meehan read Irina Medvedeva's translations of the poems of Anna Akhmatova to a packed and rapt audience, bringing tears to Irina's eyes as he read.

While he was writing his novel *The Fabulists* (Lilliput Press, 1995) he frequently sat and wrote at a window table looking out over the River Liffey. One day he asked if I had any objection to The Winding Stair being mentioned in a novel he was writing. He handed me the manuscript to read and I loved this novel in which I as well as members of The Winding Stair staff are mentioned by name. It was a proud moment and a wonderful book.

In the late 1990s Philip and I and the author Anthony Glavin formed a mischievous triumvirate that met frequently in the cafes and bars surrounding Dublin's Capel Street that was close to Philip's home. Our favourite was the snug in Hughes's pub behind the Four Courts where we would howl with tear-filled laughter and became temporary nuisances to the traditional musicians who also gathered there to play. After I sold The Winding Stair in 2006 and moved to the United States, our communications became even more frequent and hilariously funny. I became a regular traveller 'home' so we still managed to meet three or four times a year, picking up where we had left off, teasing, cajoling, sharing our joys and sorrows, our work, our love for one another. Looking at the photos that record those encounters I see us aging while being absorbed ever more deeply into a magnificent friendship.

Philip died two weeks before I returned to Ireland for good. We had been in touch until illness weakened him. I miss him. Now, when I walk the streets surrounding the quays, I expect to bump into him turning a corner, or to stop and chat with him at the Temple Bar Farmers' Market, his canvas bag brimming with cheeses and leeks, or, as I cross the Ha'Penny Bridge and glance towards The Winding Stair, in my mind's eye I see Philip, with that same brown canvas bag slung over his shoulder, leaning on his blue and yellow crutches, peering in through the window at the book display.

Philip at The Winding Stair with his friends, Kevin Connolly and Benedict Schlepper-Connolly, 1985

Tony Corbett

OUR SPANISH ADVENTURE

I met Philip Casey in Dublin in 1970 through a friend of mine, Paddy Doyle (later the author of *The God Squad*). Phil – as I always called him – was living in a bedsit at the time. I was still living with my family in Raheny. Phil and I hit it off immediately, and in no time at all we became bosom buddies. In fact, we ended up sharing a flat with Paddy called The Mews at the rear of number 46 Beechwood Avenue in Ranelagh.

What impressed me most about Phil were his qualities as a human being. He was a sensitive, generous, humble, honest and passionate man. I'll never forget the day I found him in tears. It was a late Sunday afternoon and many of us were in a state of shock on account of the shootings in Derry the very same day. There was Phil sitting on his bed with his head in his hands, uttering: *Why? Why? Why?* It was a very sad day for all of us, but the effect it had on Phil was absolutely devastating.

Some of the funniest moments we shared were at our little home, The Mews. There were unforgettable times entertaining each other when Phil recited some of his beautiful poetry for Paddy and I, or we listened to Paddy strumming a few chords on the guitar. He would break into a Kris Kristofferson or James Taylor number. Sometimes I improvised a comical sketch such as two breadcrumbs on the kitchen table having an absurd conversation while Phil and Paddy roared with laughter. Phil always laughed from the bottom of his big heart. They were wonderful times. Wonderful! And then there were the parties.

Phil and I enjoyed many adventures together in and around Dublin in the company of Paddy and other friends, but our biggest and most daring adventure around that time was our decision to leave Ireland. At first, there were six of us interested in going to Paris, but in the end it was just Phil and I who were the most daring.

I'll never forget the day we were leaving Dublin. It was mid-September 1974. We were about to head off on our biggest adventure of all. My father gave me a big hug and wished me luck on his way to work. My mum couldn't say goodbye to me. She just couldn't accept the fact that I was actually leaving.

We got the train down to Gorey and from there we went on to Hollyfort where Phil's parents had a farm. There I met his hospitable parents and little sister Karina for the first time. I had already met Phil's brothers Peter and John in Dublin, probably at one of our many parties at The Mews. We spent the night at the farm before taking the ferry the following day from Rosslare to Le Havre in the north of France.

We arrived in Paris, two very excited young Irishmen. We had done it even though several of our friends didn't think we would. But here we were in a land unknown to us! Why France? I can't quite remember really but Paris always had a special attraction for us. A fascination really! Maybe this was a dream coming true?

Phil had some knowledge of the French language, but I could only gabble 4 or 5 words. In those days there weren't as many people who spoke English as there are today. The Parisians prefer to hear you speaking French, and good French. We certainly did not impress them.

We found the city absolutely fascinating, with its wide tree-lined boulevards and beautiful architecture. We walked the streets in search of a cheap hostel, and eventually found one in the Latin Quarter. The following day we set out in search of work. We marvelled at the lovely cafés and restaurants, and gaped in admiration at the elegance of French ladies. After several days sauntering around the streets and not finding any possibility of work, we agreed that we should move on.

We decided to go somewhere cheaper so we chose Spain. We thought one of the two most important cities would be a good choice, Madrid or Barcelona. We agreed to toss a coin. Barcelona won the toss, so we grabbed our rucksacks and got on a train at Austerlitz station. We couldn't get seats on the train as it was completely full, so we just sat on the floor at one end of the carriage where we were nearly trampled to death each time the train stopped at a station.

We stopped at Portbou on the border to change over to a Spanish train, and here we had to go through Customs. The Guardia Civil policemen checked our rucksacks and to our surprise, confiscated the books we had been reading on the way down. I was reading Kafka's *Metamorphosis* and Phil was reading Jean Paul Sartre's *The Age of Reason*. We had just entered Franco's territory with books that had obviously been blacklisted in Spain. This was our introduction to the country!

We arrived at Barcelona's main station, Estación de Francia, two very tired and weary young men. Just as we were about to step off the train, a man appeared on the platform with a welcoming smile. He told us to follow him to a very cheap *pension* (hostel) not far from the station. We were so exhausted after our long journey that we followed him across the street and entered quite a decadent neighbourhood with narrow cobbled streets that had a putrid lingering odour coming from the drains. We arrived at a dilapidated building which would be our home for the following week. Today, this neighbourhood is known as El Born and is one of the most popular places in the city with its fashionable shops, bars and restaurants.

The following week we checked into a cheaper pension just off the main thoroughfare, Avenida del Marquès de l'Argentera. Here we had a small room with two beds and the use of a communal bathroom. It was not as comfortable as our previous hostel, nor did they serve meals, but we were happy enough and stayed until just before Christmas.

Phil continued writing in the hostel and sometimes read some of his work to me. I made him laugh by performing my absurd comedy acts. As I always improvised, several times he told me that I should write these things down. I should have taken his advice! Paddy told me how Phil gave him invaluable help when he wanted to get *The God Squad* published. Phil was always so kind and thoughtful. While we were here we lived on sandwiches due to our precarious finances, and only treated ourselves to a paella for lunch at a local restaurant on Sundays. After lunch we went to a nearby park called Parc de la Ciutadella where we liked to take advantage of a relaxing afternoon and read.

We had been to several English language schools looking for work. We had also been buying *La Vanguardia* newspaper as often as we could because it had the most pages dedicated to job advertisements. We continued exploring the city in search of work. One thing that both of us found quite imposing was to see armed policemen in front of government buildings with rifles or machine guns in their hands. A sight we were just not used to seeing in Ireland where the only type of weapon a uniformed policeman had was a truncheon. Then again, we were in a country ruled by a dictator.

We discovered a nice bar just round the corner from our hostel and chose it as our local. It was located in a small hotel called Park Hotel, and here we enjoyed a few beers in the evening and got to know the different people who worked there as well as the odd customer. Dimitrio and Marino were the two barmen, and Benito and Román worked in the hotel reception. Benito and Román were the only two who spoke English. Even though we didn't speak Spanish, we connected really well with Dimitrio and

Marino, possibly because they worked in the bar where we spent most of our time.

We met Ahmed, a Moroccan who spoke English quite well, and in no time we became drinking buddies. We used sign language to communicate with those who didn't understand English. Occasionally, there were arm-wrestling matches which Phil always won! We learned to play *chinos*, which was a game with at least 2 players in which you tried to guess the total number of coins the players had in their closed hands including your own, which could be 0 to 6 with only two players playing. Each player was allowed 3 coins at the most. The loser usually had to buy a round of drinks.

We eventually found work in an English academy called La Casa Inglesa in Paseo de Gracia, one of the most emblematic streets in the city. We were most impressed with this street when we first arrived, mainly due to the fact that there were so many banks. Today it's a street lined with expensive shops and restaurants where wealthy Russian and Chinese tourists do their shopping. However, it still remains the most attractive street in the city.

We discovered a lovely little bar called Bar Carabela down by the harbour. At that time Barcelona was a city with its back to the sea. However, the transformation carried out in preparation for the 1992 Olympic Games opened the city up to the sea, which was a tremendous improvement. Bar Carabela was run by a very charming man called José who spoke very good English which he had learned while working in London. Here we shared some very happy moments with José and some of his customers. We usually went to José's bar around lunchtime or just before to have an apéritif. One day he asked us if we would like to have lunch there and we discreetly told him that we couldn't afford it as we wouldn't receive our first salary till the end of the month. We had only started working at La Casa Inglesa the week before. *Come on my friends*, he said. *You can have lunch here when you want and pay me at the end of the month.* It was a generous offer which we gratefully accepted.

On the evening of December 21st we went to Park Hotel to have a few beers and wish all our friends a very Merry Christmas before going to Ireland the following day to spend Christmas with our families. We had been in Barcelona for a little over 3 months at that stage. Ahmed appeared with a large Christmas hamper for Phil and myself. It was a wonderful gesture and we couldn't hide our emotion. The drinks were on the house that night. The following day we flew back to Dublin with terrible hangovers. In those days we had to go via London as there were no direct flights to Dublin. On the flight to London and later to Dublin we met some other Irish people who were also trying to make a living in Barcelona. We exchanged phone numbers to keep in contact.

The welcome we received at Dublin Airport was unforgettable. Our families and close friends were all there waiting to receive us with open arms. Our friends were carrying a placard that read "WELCOME HOME PHIL AND TONY!" Our emotions got the better of us. My mother stepped forward and hugged me saying: *I wanted to be the first, son.* We were receiving a heroes' welcome.

After Christmas we moved into an apartment in Sagrada Familia, sharing with one of the friends we had made on the flight over to Dublin. Life became more comfortable, and we started to get to know more people from all walks of life. But that is another story.

Phil stayed on in Barcelona for another three years. Eventually he decided to go back to Ireland where his source of inspiration was so much stronger, and from where he wrote the bulk of his most appreciated work. I feel privileged to have had the opportunity to have spent so much time in the company of such a fascinating human being.

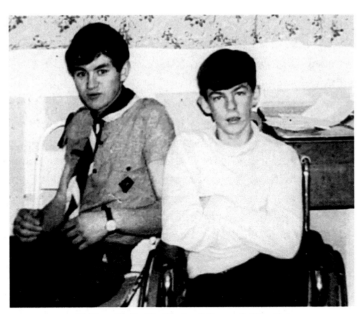

Philip with Paddy Doyle at Cappagh Hospital

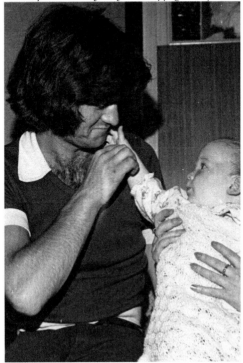

Philip with Paddy Doyle's son, Shane

Patrick Cotter

THE COMFORTING PLEASURES OF SADNESS

The Minister lived like a perverse King Midas;
everything he touched turned to lies.
"Policemen wave wands not truncheons.

They are fairy godparents to the unemployed.
In place of cars we give them melons.
In place of steeds we give them vermin.

The unemployed, like children, are our treasured
possessions. Their innocence in the face
of adversity, their meekness before hardship

instills the More Fortunate with paternal-like
pleasures. The jobless, like children, are our much
beloved. They bejewel us with simple pride

in our situation. They bestow on us granaries
of gratitude, dowries of deliverance, vaults
of vicissimathunk."

The Minister's dark limousine was disguised
as a crystal carriage before the people's eyes;
his axe swing was a smooth caress, his drown

-ings were presented as baptisms. And so
the lies were spun like a noose.
"Sadnesses do not exist and where they do

they are pleasurable, as pleasurable as dark
-ness, and loneliness, silence and bleeding."
On the health of the nation he intoned:

"Measles is administered to preserve traditional
childhood. Cancer is dispensed to the people
to make our every day more valued."

His darkest abode was made to seem white
as wedding cake. His richest suit a holy man's
vestments. His minions told the people:

"The Minister is so close to God in his house
he has clouds instead of carpets.
And we have seen him make cake out of words.

In his eyes he absorbs all the sadnesses
of the world. Through his heart is pumped
everyone's love of the earth."

Thus did *The Comforting Pleasures of Sadness*
come to be spun like a noose
unravelled like a wound.

1989

Tony Curtis

TWO VISIONS OF PHILIP

Poetry, it's still the best way
of talking to the dead.
– W.H. Auden

Though you are gone five years,
every time I cross the Ha'penny Bridge
I see you coming towards me:
long scarf, big bag, bright smile,
everything tilted except for the smile
and, of course, the sweetness
                of seeing you again.

They tell me the dead
are always listening,
so I suppose you heard
I sang *The Parting Glass*
at your memorial in Hollyfort.
Philip, it's a song that could
have been written just for you:

      Of all the friends that ever I had
      They are sorry for my going away
      And all the sweethearts ever I had
      They'd wish me one more day to stay.

These days when I think of you,
I think of a contented soul
sitting in the sun, playing a banjo:
country, carefree, right foot
tapping out a rhythm that flows
as naturally as a mountain stream.

You always lived close to rivers
but the truth is you were
more cello than banjo,
your sonorous voice, autumnal.
Whenever we spoke,
I could feel leaves falling,
the stillness of the river fading into night.

Katie Donovan

THE NIGHT FOR PHILIP, 2015

"One of the most beloved of contemporary poets" is how Ireland Professor of Poetry, Paula Meehan, describes Philip Casey. Poet, novelist and member of Aosdána, Philip Casey will be honoured by friends, family and the Irish literary community tonight in the Oak Room of the Mansion House when a launch of his *Selected Poems* will take place.

Co-hosted by Dermot Bolger and myself, this event will celebrate Casey's many achievements, including five collections of poetry and four novels. Casey is also the founder and editor of the website Irish Writers Online, which provides biographical details of Irish writers. A free resource, it is used worldwide.

Casey's vision is both local and international. He spent several years living in Barcelona and has connections in Germany where he still is a regular visitor (his play, *Cardinal*, was produced in Hamburg in 1990). He was born to Irish parents (Laois and Sligo) in London in 1950 but spent formative years on a farm in Hollyfort, County Wexford. He has long been based in central Dublin and is a familiar figure at literary events, which he attends with determined loyalty.

His spare, elegiac poetry gives voice to themes of family, place, love in its many forms, political injustice, and pain, both physical and emotional. Casey lost a leg due to complications following intense radiation to treat cancer. He began writing verse by first of all composing songs with a guitar as a teenager in his hospital bed. His perspective is one of wry, hard-won insight, suggesting passion and suffering by restraint rather than overspill.

That Casey is held in high regard by his peers is reflected in the fact that tonight's event could not be opened to the public due to limitations of space, because so many of Casey's literary colleagues wanted to be there in person to celebrate the man and the work.

Guests include the novelists Sebastian Barry and Joe O'Connor, the artists Alice Maher and Dermot Seymour as well as poets Paula Meehan, Eiléan Ní Chuilleanáin, Macdara Woods, Pat Boran, Gerard Smyth, Mary O'Donnell and many more. A few of the guests, including poets Aidan Murphy, Heather Brett and Terry McDonagh, will read poems by Casey which have personal resonances for them, as will friends and family members. German guest Ulrike Boskamp and her daughter, Klara, who have flown in from Berlin, will each read a poem that has been dedicated to them.

Philip Casey's first collection of poetry, *Those Distant Summers*, was published in 1980 by Raven Arts Press and is heavily influenced by his youth on a farm in Hollyfort. *The curlew cried in the bog before a band of rain came from Croghan like an animal*, he recalls. *It sank a deep well in my imagination*. Tonight several of his Wexford friends will be present, including Sean and Kay Halford, who will also read a poem.

Tried and Sentenced is edited by Marion Kelly and includes a selection of poems from all four of Casey's collections (the other three are *After Thunder* and *The Year of the Knife*, both published by Raven; and *Dialogue in Fading Light*, published by New Island). "Things that please me in poetry are precision, compassion and images that surpass the common run of language; also that the poet must have an ear for language as a musician has an ear for music," wrote Michael Hartnett, in a review of *The Year of the Knife*. "The work of Philip Casey possesses all of these in abundance."

Launching Casey's *Selected Poems* tonight is writer Ronan Sheehan, who reviewed Casey's first novel, *The Fabulists* (1994), with the following: "This is a passionate, erotic, mature novel that displays many of the virtues which contemporary Irish fiction so conspicuously lacks: an intelligent vision of an adult relationship coupled with an intelligent vision of contemporary Irish society. Plus he has a supple prose style which is a constant joy to read."

Casey's trilogy of novels began with *The Fabulists*, first published by Antony Farrell's Lilliput Press, which won the inaugural Listowel Writers' Week Novel of the Year award in 1995, and earned praise from Martha Gellhorn and Colm Tóibín (who called it "a stunningly truthful and perfectly pitched novel"). The novel features a pair of Dublin lovers who are struggling with poverty and family ties, wooing each other with invented tales of cosmopolitan wanderings.

The Water Star (Picador, 1999) and *The Fisher Child* (Picador, 2001) completed what is now the Bann River Trilogy, encompassing Casey's much-loved landscape of North Wexford, as well as the Irish diaspora in London (which Casey experienced firsthand – some of his earliest memories are of playing in bombsites in Highgate); how families evolve and survive through turmoil and suppressed secrets; and the terrible legacy of slavery. From the intimate streets of pre-boom Dublin where *The Fabulists* begins, Casey opens his fiction to international dimensions, most ambitiously in the historical strands of *The Fisher Child*, which moves from scenes of 1798 fighting in Wexford to the Irish owned slave plantations in Montserrat.

As mainstream publishing struggles to adapt to a changing world, Casey has taken back ownership of his printed works, like many writers and musicians, seeking greater creative control and using his considerable expertise with technology. He established eMaker Editions, an independent imprint, to make his work available globally as ebooks on kindle and as print-on-demand editions via Amazon, the Book Depository and

Barnes & Noble. In Ireland his books can be found in Books Upstairs (Dublin), Kennys (Galway), and Zozimus Books (Gorey).

I first met Philip Casey through the late lamented James Liddy and Paul Funge, who together produced the pioneering but now sadly defunct Gorey Arts Festival and its spin-off, the wonderfully named *Gorey Detail* literary magazine. Philip was one of several Wexford poets I met through James Liddy and the festival, including Eamonn Wall, Paddy Kehoe and Mick Considine (who will attend tonight). As a newbie teenage poet, I was delighted to be a satellite of such fun-filled, exciting company. Although it is decades hence, I have the same feeling about tonight.

TRIBUTES TO PHILIP

Dermot Bolger, novelist and poet:
Since his debut collection in 1980, Philip Casey has been a treasured author who has enriched Irish writing not only through his acclaimed poetry collections and celebrated Bann River Trilogy of novels, but also through his pioneering works on behalf of Irish writing. These include the famous Irish Writers Online website, which he originated and has maintained as a free online resource and is used worldwide. Tonight we salute his contribution to the cultural life of Dublin as well as his new book *Tried and Sentenced: Selected Poems*, which showcases one of Irish writing's most esteemed voices. Casey is an essential presence in Irish writing over the past quarter century.

Eiléan Ní Chuilleanáin, poet:
Philip Casey has been a wise, joyful presence among Irish writers, a devoted chronicler and adviser, innovative and courageous in literature as in life. It's great to revisit his poetry and to have an opportunity to celebrate the most

important thing, his outstanding creative achievement, with the publication of *Tried and Sentenced*.

Thomas Lynch, poet and essayist:
After we are all gone to ground again, Philip Casey's work in words will be happily haunting new readers and old ones. His fictions and poems ennoble the species and the art. Quite apart from his own writerly output is his work in service of other writers, early on taming the frontiers of daunting new technologies to lengthen the table of our community. Philip Casey is that rare gift among his fellows – a poet and fictionist free of ego or selfish impulse, generous by nature, genial in aspect and graceful in praxis: a gift.

Maureen Kennelly, director of Poetry Ireland:
The publication of Philip Casey's *Selected Poems* offers a wonderful opportunity to remind us of his many poetic achievements which have maybe been overshadowed in more recent years by his prose. And it's an occasion to celebrate the very rich part that he continues to play in Dublin's poetry landscape.

Paula Meehan, Ireland Professor of Poetry:
Philip Casey is one of the most beloved of contemporary poets. His compassion, his courage and his great gift for friendship are valued by his fellow poets nearly as much as we value the wisdom and humanity of the lyric poetry he makes. In his novels he has delineated the soul's journey towards integration in the face of cultural and historical disintegration. In his pioneering work on the internet and as an activist, he has served all that is good and liberating in a lifelong search for truth and justice.

Gerard Smyth, poet:
Before I met him, which must have been through that gatherer of poets, James Liddy, I had read his bulletins from the land of Lorca. Unlike myself at the time, Philip had been off to experience exotic places and brought back those places in the lyrical and exquisite poems of his debut collection *Those Distant Summers*: The Chamartin-Barcelona Termino Express, Missing a Lady in Calle Padua, La Extranjera. The long-haired Philip I first met during a distant summer of the early 1970s stills beams his broad lovely smile from the back cover of that book that so impressed me. The hair may now be a bit shorter but the smile is the same whenever we meet. Like the poet himself, his poems are a blend of tenderness and fortitude. All these years later his old songs make their way to my heart.

Antony Farrell, editor of Lilliput Press:
Lilliput Press was thrilled and proud to publish *The Fabulists*, Philip Casey's pre-Tiger first novel in the mid-nineties, reflecting a cosmopolitan Dublin of hope and futurity, contemporaneous and emotionally engaged in the spell of its protagonists Tess and Mungo. Launched by Sebastian Barry, it won critical acclaim, and went on to win the Listowel Writers' Week novel of the year 1995. A coming of age for us all.

Philip Casey

AN INDIAN DREAMS OF THE RIVER
for Terry and Kevin

I can no longer smell freedom on the river.
A woman's life is always hard,
but at least I had my teeth, then.

My smile was famous in the village.
They have polluted my river
with the burning leather
of their jackboots.
At night, when the fireflies eat my brain,
I think of how they broke my husband,
bone by white bone.
Curse by obscene curse they raped me,
clutching José's swollen eyes open
to see our shame.
I cannot eat fish anymore
because they remind me of their eyes.
Sleep comes like a caravel of *Conquistadores*,
gleaming Toledo bayonets flecked with blood.

Philip speaking at The Mansion House

Theo Dorgan

REMEMBERING PHILIP CASEY
THAT FIERCE AND GENTLE MAN

I may have been thinking of John Keats, dead at 25, when I should have been thinking about Robert Frost, who didn't publish his first collection until aged 40 or so. Thus, the impatience of the young poet, eager, too eager, to see a book in print.

Whatever the reason, I sent off what I fondly hoped would be my first collection while still enrolled for an MA in UCC. Give Dermot Bolger his due (and I am always happy to salute that lovely man), he didn't keep me waiting too long for a reply. Tactful and considerate, he turned down the opportunity to unleash my juvenile talent on the world with kindness and courtesy, suggesting that I consider the enclosed reader's report carefully; if I were of a mind to do so, he wrote, I might care to send on some later version of the manuscript when I'd had time to rework it.

The reader's report, when I'd got over myself enough to read it, was a model of its kind — considered, thoughtful, professionally merciless, written with close and meticulous attention to the poems as they stood naked on the page. It was signed, Philip Casey.

I had seen some of his poems here and there, I knew little of the man, but when I saw that signature at the end of the report I knew at once we would be friends.

Not, necessarily, that I agreed with his criticisms, for criticisms there were in dismaying plenty, not at first. Nor did I know enough to give any great credence to his words of praise for certain poems, phrases or turns of craft. Not immediately, anyway, although as I calmed down I began to understand with gratitude the quality of his perceptions and advice.

No, what struck me most forcibly on that first impression was the sheer decency of his having signed his name, the qualities of professional courtesy, confidence and personal courage implicit in that simple act.

We did indeed become friends, and my admiration for Philip's innate sense of tact, his intelligence and straightforward goodness of heart, only grew with time. As did my admiration for the earned authority and grace of his work as poet and novelist. I was fortunate indeed to benefit from that authority in its youthful manifestation – his reading of those early poems taught me so many lessons that have stood to me down the years, even if I was to prove something of a slow learner. I learned from him that first, most crucial, lesson all young poets need to take to heart — the words on the page must fend for themselves once the author has lifted her or his hand. Philip read what I had written, just that, unswayed by any special pleading I might have offered. He was cold and clear where it was needed, and unafraid — and by being just that he allowed me to learn, having meditated on the business, that I, too, had to stand outside the work, had to learn to let the poem stand on its own two feet.

And for all that, he was gentle.

Nobody likes being knocked back, and few who go on to make a life in the craft can or will pretend that having your work returned — let's be blunt, rejected — is a pleasant experience. Especially so for a young poet, riddled with carefully-hidden doubts and insecurities, hidden perhaps most of all from herself or himself. I have always been grateful that Dermot gave that first manuscript to Philip, and that Philip put his name to that report. Somehow, and to this day I'm not quite sure why, it was the simple fact of that signature that allowed me to overcome ego-hurt and to look at the work as he had looked at it, square in the face.

In the long years of our friendship after, some imp of misrule would prompt me, now and again, to bring this up with him. All those who knew Philip, and loved him, will remember that slow smile of his, that shrewd, mischievous look up from under his brow that presaged some devilment or other: *Ah sure*, he'd say, *there's always room for improvement in this life*. And then that irrepressible, helpless, burst of laughter. Salud, Philip, and thank you. You were some man for one man.

Anthony Glavin

A TREASURED FRIENDSHIP

I first met Philip Casey in the spring of 1995, having received a lovely card from him following my *Sunday Tribune* review of his stellar first novel, *The Fabulists*, whose riveting love story of Dublin, underpinned by a persuasive spiritual dimension, proved a singular, stunning tale. A treasured friendship then quickly followed, with numerous afternoons and evenings either within his Arran Street East, Dublin home, the nearby Hughes pub, or his favourite bookshop-cum-cafe, The Winding Stair, whose founding proprietor, Kevin Connolly, was himself a dear friend of Philip. Philip's years in Barcelona, and my own in the US Peace Corps in Costa Rica, had bequeathed us both with sufficient Spanish to occasionally, never mind jovially, converse about another party in our company. Yet tables might then turn – as tables do – should the conversation wax *as Gaeilge*, or with Don Felipe and Kevin Connolly breaking into laughter at my *C'mon here to me ... This'll be quick!* – as if a Yank might ever manage to be quick with yet another yarn. Only for Philip to then suggest how those same seven words might themselves serve as the start of a story. *Just let the spoken voice do the work,* he sagely advised. *Record yourself, as it were. The power of how one tells a tale is in the voice. No middle-man, no ornamentation. Write it as you speak it.* Tables were also employed chez Arran Street East for a reading of Tarot cards or I-Ching divinations, given Philip's own openness to a range of augury pathways, though the latter thankfully proceeded via the throwing of three French francs, not fifty yarrow stalks. Supper was also similarly served on various occasions, and I can picture Philip's kitchen yet, wherein one of us generally managed to have the dishes done ahead of our dear host.

And yes, tables might also feature a range of cocktails from Mojitos to Sombreros, albeit always within reason, given that I'd be cycling home to Whitehall, whatever about once offering a crossbar to a fellow guest, which had me finally hitting the hay *chez moi* at 4am.

Among the many joys of reading a book that you'll go on to treasure is the manner in which the locale wherein you first encounter it might intertwine with your memory of the tale itself. And so it was, during a short holiday in a wee chalet overlooking the Silver Strand in Malinbeg, County Donegal in August of 1998, that I dove into Philip's acclaimed novel *The Water Star* with its radiant, 1950s, post-war London exploration of family, isolation, love, loss and hope. A storyline which moved me to tears with its compelling depiction of how parents, siblings, friends and past lovers can somehow manage against considerable odds to share what the Irish poet AE once described as our spiritual journey. A journey on which our dear Irish poet and novelist Philip Casey himself continues to cast the brightest, most benevolent light.

And I was once again seaside in Doolin, County Clare, on the 5th of February 2018, where having wished upon a northern star above its pier that all of Philip's breaths to come might prove gentle ones, I then took a phone call from my partner Adrienne, with the saddest word of Philip having crossed over to the other side the previous day. And as the Luas neared Hughes Pub the following afternoon, my tears fell once more. Yet *landscape gives back memories* as the poet Philip himself wrote, and this same swathe of Northside Dublin remains awash with the warmest, brightest and beloved to this day.

Maeve Hickey

Fado for Philip

acrylic and fabric on canvas

Patrick Kehoe

PHILIP CASEY
A POEM IN MEMORY

I always loved the opening lines here, now serving as epigraph for my poem, with their quiet note of certainty and promise to oneself. I love their declaration of intent and self-preservation, their reckoning with the immediate future in a young man's life, a decision of some moment.

Philip lived near Plaza Lesseps, I believe, on Calle Padua. I lived relatively nearby in a pensión on Mayor de Gracia during the first weeks. However, we did not coincide in Barcelona, I came in 1978 after he had left in 1977.

Yet it was the same city, of cheap hotels (and a few luxurious hotels and restaurants that were out of reach), bars that were also eateries, of trains and buses on their loops throughout the day and much of the night. City of lottery ticket sellers endlessly proclaiming their wares, vendors of sunflower seeds and peanuts, decent working men and women.

I think of him there, trying to make a living, commuting in the bustling, often over-heated city. Falling in love maybe, thinking of home no doubt and the green fields of Wexford, the generally wetter, muckier landscape he grew up in. I can assume certain things about his life there.

As it happened, I came shortly after both he and his friend and fellow poet, the late Gerry Fanning, had left Barcelona. Yet I know that the leaving of such an addictive place, to return to a very different, more indolent and relatively easy-going Ireland, was no easy matter in those years.

The arrival was a much better experience, I might surmise, if a bracing one. Typically, there was a vagueness about the English classes materialising at all, at the very start of one's teaching sojourn. We were there ultimately on a wing and a prayer.

When I came back from Spain in 1977, I was a round peg in a square hole, so about two years later I decided to do what I'd always wanted to do, which was to write poems. Philip Casey, quoting from a 2013 online interview with Katie O'Reilly.

PLAZA LESSEPS AND ENVIRONS

I'll sleep.
Tomorrow blue water
will bring me home
and I'll rest
– Philip Casey

I am always going up to Príncipe de Asturias,
To Plaza Lesseps, its metro station and ragged plaza;
The broad sweep of Ronda General Mitre,
The creeping ivy of the names,
1978, when the world knew itself

And needed no satellite death-in-life
To find its way around. Streets were found
By asking questions in Castellano;
The mystery of the language adhered,
Furtively you climbed into its grotto and rock patterns,

And even slept there, curled up on a shelf
of unfamiliar syntax.
In my mind, like Philip Casey's blue water
Bringing him home, I am going the other way,
Into Avenida del Tibidabo, the brass slumber
Of summer jazz, Kenny Dorham, Art Blakey

Hoping my number comes up,
Hoping the hat-check lady, the Bebop lady

Hands me back a different, dashing coat,
Forgetting the cold returns later, that evening on Marina,
The mind's engine flooded with frost, remembering.

I am always going up and over,
Tripping myself over dented trombones,
Trumpets clear as the gushing water in Plaza de España.

James Liddy, Dermot Bolger, Philip Casey, Kay Halford, Michael Considine, Eamonn Wall and Seán Clerkin at the launch of Wexford Through its Writers, *edited by Dermot Bolger (New Island Books, 1992), Woodlands Gallery, Kilanerin, County Wexford*

THE BARD OF ARRAN STREET EAST

Philip's friendship was an immeasurable gift. Where to begin writing about my ally, my lost comrade?

My quest takes me first to Nerja, Spain, the location for Aidan Higgins' Booker shortlisted novel, *Balcony of Europe*. Philip impressed upon me the significance of the novel for his generation of writers. One of the earliest gifts I received from him was a beautiful copy of this book. Some of my best memories of Philip have a Spanish connection: the way his face lit up as he sampled his favourite Spanish wine, Rioja, at the beginning of a meal and how, regularly, at the end of an evening, he would recite Antonio Machado's poems with great feeling. Michael Hartnett's translations of Federico García Lorca's *Gypsy Ballads* were referred to in almost any discussion of translation, and often accompanied by a recitation. Hartnett provided an imaginative link to my own background in Sliabh Luachra, so these performances fascinated me.

I first met Philip in 2008 when I interviewed him for my radio show, "The Parlour Review", on Dublin City FM. I had read *The Water Star* soon after reading Timothy O'Grady's *I Could Read the Sky*. Both novels captured something essential about the Irish experience of emigration and exile in twentieth-century London. *The Water Star* is a sensitive treatment of the plight of Irish immigrants adjusting to life in London. The early chapters paint a harrowing picture of poverty, loss and the effects of inter-generational trauma on a father and son.

There is a sense in which the eponymous passage of *The Water Star*, which details Hugh's flight from his father and the weight of their shared past, becomes a metaphor for Philip's journey. The dereliction of the bomb site Hugh shelters in, combined with his emotional turmoil, transitions into something mystical and redemptive. These passages, set in post-war London, have a quietly Blakean character. There is a reaching heavenwards, but in Philip's case the supernatural is resisted, the galaxy itself sufficient to delight his senses:

> Although in the centre of what had been the building, it was exposed, where the roof had collapsed through three floors. The rain had stopped and the sky was clearing, and a fresh star blinked at him as a cloud moved away. He blinked back at it, lost in its beauty. As he turned away, he realized that his face was a few inches from a pool of water. He glanced at the sky and then back, enchanted that it was starlight which danced fuzzily in the pool, and then gazed at the star again, losing himself in contemplation of its lonely station up there in the galaxy.
>
> 'O water star ...' he whispered.

Reading Philip's novels again after his death, I am struck by the way that he transformed the elements of his life into art. It would do him a disservice to break down the elements sociologically because his sensitivity to metaphor was something altogether more elemental. He combined his own experience of physical pain with his articulation of human suffering. The lost potential of the United Irishmen and the failure of the 1798 rebellion was a subject he returned to over and over again. His imaginative engagement with the suffering that ensued transcends any straightforward recording of the facts. In *The Fisher Child* he enters into the mind of a Wexford rebel at the height of the pitched battles. Philip never flinched in his description of the reality of war, colonisation and subjugation.

The three works that make up the Bann River Trilogy contain themes that would hold Philip's imagination for a lifetime, and much of the psychological and historical questions that pressed on his thought are worked out through characters in those novels. Reading *The Water Star*,

I understood why he marvelled at his father's ability to recite part of the Latin mass when he was close to death "letting the flow of Latin drug him". Philip had an understanding of the grace of benediction, in his case, "secular prayer", and the capacity of ritualised language to comfort a soul in distress. He often praised the language of the St James Bible and quoted from the Pauline epistle: "For now we see through a glass, darkly; but then face to face: now I know in part; but then shall I know even as also I am known."

A striking feature of Philip's novels is his characterisation of the transformative nature of human intimacy, the importance of finding a language to express suffering in, and ultimately, the redemptive nature of the act of witnessing and holding another's pain. A recurring motif is listening as a political act. Anyone who knew Philip knew that, in the realm of listening, he was sovereign: "Hugh listened to her and was never impatient."

Philip was impressed by Jean-Paul Sartre's notion of the committed writer and Sartre's attempts to reconcile existentialism with Marxism. His own commitment was to the truth of felt experience. This is a remarkable feature of *The Water Star*. It's hard not to conclude that Philip was writing from his own experience in the following extract:

> There could have been a lead weight on his foot, and when he got back on the bed he cupped his ankle in his hands. The bandage was thick and protective, and he felt the pain was much further away from his fingers than it was, and that if only he could touch the flesh he could soothe it ... His ankle was throbbing, so he sat on the edge of the bed, hoping that putting his foot on the cool floor would relieve it. He tried raising it against the headboard, his reasoning being that if the blood flowed away, the pain would also flow away. He yawned, caught between exhaustion and his insistent ankle, and he stayed awake like that, his thoughts straying through random images until they were

pulled back to his pain. There was no escape. The hours passed and dawn came, and the birds sang with it. He was past yawning now, his eyes as heavy as his ankle.

The passage is an acute rendering of how illness distorts the concept of time and duration, and even the bird, nature's redeeming presence, is unable to penetrate the fog of pain. The following passage from *The Water Star* describes acute pain with anatomical precision. Hugh suffers a serious lime burn after fresh cement comes in contact with his skin:

He put his foot on the ground again. It throbbed so heavily that his heart pounded, but he had to walk. Nature was calling. He stood, and almost immediately gave up. At first, he tensed his body, trying to defeat the burning, but when that seemed only to magnify it, he tried with an equal will to relax, to become detached from it, to let it be. This worked up to a point, but needed concentration; yet he managed it, somehow, even as he dressed.

These passages in the novel give way to the joy of being cared for, of recovery, of the redemptive quality of miracles taken for granted in everyday life: "It struck him that walking was a miracle all of its own."

One of the things I admired about Philip was the fact that he was never entirely at home with the political environment taking shape around him. He spent his days studying power structures, imperialism, the language of power, mythmaking - making multiple case studies of the legacy of various historical figures. In light of our conversations, I founded a club called The Funks of the Screw. It was inspired by the Monks of The Screw, an eighteenth-century drinking club founded by John Philpott Curran. We drew up our mission statement:

The Funks are dedicated to the brilliant and the bold of Ireland's past, luminaries often misunderstood or forgotten. With an emphasis on conversation, commentary, and friendship, the Funks seek to emulate the conviviality of their eighteenth-century exemplars The Monks of the Screw, who 'mingled mirth with wisdom and gave to political philosophy the charm of eloquence'.

We wanted to animate certain historical figures and highlight what they might say to us today. Philip was drawing on his gift for crafting a good story to convey the importance of certain individuals in the development of Ireland's *Res publica*. He delighted in recounting the exploits of William Lamport, the seventeenth-century Wexford prodigy who escaped a pirate ship and became a skilled propagandist for the Spanish court. Lamport was ultimately sentenced to death in Mexico after seventeen years in an Inquisition jail for his outspoken criticism of the Spanish colonisers.

The peregrinations of Thomas Russell, the correspondence between William Drennan and his sister Martha McTier, and the trenchant polemic of John Toland were daily sources of inspiration for Philip. I prize his copy of *The Man from God Knows Where: Thomas Russell, 1767–1803*, which was always close to hand on his desk. He was drawn to Peter Linebaugh's work on the efforts of local people on behalf of the United Irishmen who had been jailed for their efforts to assist the oppressed. One passage detailed the "hasty diggings" organised by the United Irishmen when a large group of men and women came together and "dug Sam Nielson's potatoes in seven minutes". Philip dwelt on Linebaugh's observation that: "That was the place where subsistence solidarity was exercised, with its alternative values to those of Bank, palanquin, and scaffold."

There was a lot of laughter as we made an eighteenth-century vernacular our own, much talk of "going forward in the right spirit" and "evidence being accepted in the court of The Master of The Rolls." Ronan Sheehan, a self-professed "Shackleton of the soul", brought legitimacy to proceedings through his connection to Philpott Curran.

Philip celebrated Michaelmas by leaving a glass of Green Spot whiskey on his window sill. We had founded the Funks with a toast to Curran's paean: "The green spot that blooms o'er the desert of life."

Philip reflected the bardic tradition in his ability to remember and pass on stories. He spoke with some veneration of the position of the *fili* and the druids in pre-Christian Ireland. One of my most memorable birthdays was celebrated around his dinner table with the artist Jesse Jones and writer Anthony Colclough. Philip animated the evening with stirring accounts of the trials and tribulations of the Bardic schools. We were like assembled time travellers, Philip a contemporary Virgil guiding us through the shades.

From about 2012 onwards, the historian Fergus Whelan became a regular guest. How this came about is a classic illustration of Philip's generosity. Philip read Whelan's book, *Dissent into Treason: Unitarians, King-killers and the Society of the United Irishman* and was so impressed that he made it his business to go to Books Upstairs and buy several copies to distribute among friends. Whelan brought many of the subjects to life with soulful renditions of songs associated with different battles and spirited accounts of enlightenment figures like Francis Hutcheson and the United Irishman Oliver Bond.

The etymology of Philip's name, with all its connotations, Philo, lover of, strikes one who knew him as absurdly true. Loved and loving. I wonder if there was anything in this world that he found mundane. When Philip was free of nerve pain his afternoons and evenings were a kaleidoscope of literary and social engagements. He drank in life's pleasures with fervour. He was seldom guilty about time wasted and there was a silent intensity to his experience of even life's simple pleasures, candlelight, the re-filling of a glass. I often felt touched by his engagement with the world, for it seemed to provide a healthy contrast to the other side of his character, the writer who laboured to counter injustice and illuminate historic patterns of conceit, originating in false ideas of nation and race. Kate O'Brien's notion that "you must write for the world" was certainly true of Philip.

I was honoured when Philip asked me to edit *Tried and Sentenced*, his *Selected Poems* that he went on to publish with eMaker Editions in 2014. I advised him to pare down the poems, heightening the starkness of his work. Philip's poetry was an exploration of how the world met him in country fields, in hospital wards, on trains. His poems fused around impressions deeply made. He once told me that on opening the fridge and seeing bottles of kefir, an image seized hold of him that brought a dream back into his waking consciousness. The whiteness had triggered a complex of images, and from there it was a matter of working out how those images would cohere on the page. I often wondered if his quiet industry was an act of defiance. Through word and code, he could overcome the world he periodically lived in, where physical pain took hold of him.

Philip's frequent experiences of hospital sensitised him to the twilight zone between waking and dreams that writers like Roland Barthes and Thomas Mann describe so well. *Tried and Sentenced* foregrounds the dimmed lights of wards at night, the flickering machines, vast corridors of weightlessness: "Torn sonatas of distress" and "The sleepless Reich of phantom pain". There is a mythical quality to Philip's hospital poems. The poet is visualised as being dropped from the pale Queen's "purse of death" into the endeavour of rebirth. Purse suggests both a container and containment, the pursed lips of suffering.

Philip was all too ready to play down his personal suffering, offsetting people's sympathy with a fine-tuned witticism. It was easy to forget in his company that moving around was harder for him than others. Once he astonished me by relaying the calculations involved in terms of expenditure of energy, laughing even then at his predicament. He didn't give in easily. I recall the daily refrain: "I must settle back into work."

Philip frequently drew my attention to the science behind the Fibonacci sequence, marvelling at the structure of the ear and spirals in the natural world. Looking back, I wonder if he took this pattern as a sign that the world was fundamentally aligned to the beautiful and its political correlate, the good, like a modern-day Pythagoras in search of illuminating metaphorical insight.

It pains me to reflect on the reality that his last years were blighted by the resurgence of crude populism and nativism, most spectacularly with the rise of Trump in the US. It hurt him deeply, and as he became progressively weaker he decided to avoid any discussion related to this subject. In 2015 he flirted with beginning another novel based on his grand-uncle's life in New York. The provisional title was *The Doorman of the Hotel Astor*, and for the short time he contemplated a new departure, it seemed to bring him renewed energy and vitality. This renewed vigour, however, led to a last charge at finishing *Histories of the Irish*, a conversation about "Irish slaves, servants, masters, traders and campaigners for emancipation." It was Philip's desire to shed light on historical abuse that brought him to explore Ireland's complicity in slavery practices. It seemed that the act of writing and witnessing was redemptive.

Philip frequently eulogised John Keats's notion of negative capability, that of "being in uncertainties, mysteries, doubts, without any irritable reaching after fact and reason", and yet this co-existed with a marvelling at scientific discovery and technological advances. He was, at heart, an optimist and conversation with him often gravitated to his belief in the next generation. He was deeply political, at one point writing a manifesto with a view to forming a political party, a well-thought-out text that foreshadowed contemporary eco-socialist politics. In his day-to-day life he was the embodiment of the Greek concept of *Arête*. His advocacy of environmental sustainability began at home and knew no bounds. I can still see in my mind's eye the rows of glass bottles for recycling on his kitchen sink, the piles of recycled elephant dung for firewood, and the environmentally friendly phone. He proudly drew one's attention to such things and explained how he discovered the initiatives, and science, behind them.

One of my lasting images of Philip is from his recollection of something that moved him deeply in São Paulo. After reading from *The Fisher Child* he found himself in a room with a number of students seated on the floor around him. He was touched by their questions and their understanding of the importance of the themes addressed in the novel. He felt that it was the task of every generation to take up the fight that was never won. He never sought mastery. In fact, he was repelled by the very nature of the master-student paradigm, and spoke warmly of Jean-Joseph Jacotot's writings on intellectual emancipation. Yet, I felt that those students were no different from the rest of us who sat around Philip divining the good we found in him.

I will finish by returning to Spain. Philip, ever conscious of his own mortality, was very moved after translating Lorca's "Horseman Song":

> Death is watching me
> From the towers of Córdoba.
> Oh the road is so long!
> Oh my courageous pony!
> Oh death waits for me
> before I reach Córdoba!

Maureen Kennelly

AT THE HEART OF IT ALL

My abiding memory of Philip Casey was of his friendliness and openness, and I'm forever grateful to him for the welcome that he showed to me. This was in the literary scene of 1990s Dublin which for me held much enchantment and mystery. Back then, the Irish Writers Centre was in its infancy and there was a lively roster of readings by a whole host of great writers – those were the evenings you'd encounter Eithne Strong, Eoin McNamee, Emer Martin and Mary O'Donnell, amongst many others. Beaming at the heart of it all was Philip who radiated kindness and fun and intelligence. I have no doubt that I am not alone in being drawn to these circles because of his openness and kindness.

A few years on, I was working with Jim Culleton in Fishamble Theatre Company and we were engaged in the delightful exercise of dreaming up names of people who might like to write a play for us. I ventured Philip's name – he'd drawn such terrific characters in Tess and Mungo in his novel *The Fabulists* that I thought a play was well within his purview. The plan came to naught in the end but all our interactions were filled with grace and humour and imaginative energy. Revisiting *The Fabulists*, I'm struck by how brilliantly he's reflected 1980s Dublin – it's a book that deserves to be better known.

Sometimes Philip attached words of wisdom from others to the end of his emails. In recent years, he used a line from Ian McLaren: *Be kind, for everyone you meet is fighting a hard battle.*

He drew from his own boundless well of kindness, affecting so many of us in countless, enduring ways. My last visual memory of him is from 11 Parnell Square where he was a sure supporter of Poetry Ireland and of our plans to make the first national centre dedicated to poetry. Down the corridor he'd come towards me, always beaming, casting his love and fun towards all of us.

Adrian Kenny

Philip Casey

I first met Philip at a Gorey Arts Festival, and knew him until he died, but my clearest memories of him are his visits on Christmas Eve. Ruth, my wife, would have been still at work in Books Upstairs when he walked over from his flat in Longwood Avenue with presents for our two daughters. They were very young, and usually had gone to bed. The two presents, wrapped in bright paper, were put under the tree, then he sat on a kitchen chair and had tea by the fire.

Though he was often in pain, his strong chest and voice showed determination. He could be angry – cursing some editor in the *Irish Press* who had dismissed a piece he had written; or describing the parish priest who drove up to his father's farm like a landlord to demand the Easter dues. In other ways he had a resigned tolerance – he gave his deep laugh when he described the patter of rats under the floorboards above his bedroom ceiling. For some reason I forget he never said a hard word against that landlord.

We used to talk about writing, and Spain, where he had worked, and Germany, where he had travelled. He had known the world, and kept a great openness. One evening he spoke lovingly about a woman he had met. When I asked about her another time, he said she had met someone else. There was dignity in what he left unsaid.

When he moved to Arran Street, I didn't see him so often, but I followed his Irish writers online website, enough work for anyone in the whole of their health. His energy may have come from knowing his good times were precious. He worked until the end at a long history of slavery. That sympathy for the defenceless was like his kindness to children. He wasn't there on Christmas morning when my two daughters opened his bright presents.

Brian Lynch

Intent on Chivalry

When I was asked to contribute to this book I was editing my own book, *Bury The Dust – A Zen Diary*, and had just come to the entry for Monday, 14 January 1999. It begins, 'Yesterday was a sad, funny, terrible day.'

The fun was lunch with Philip at Michael Hartnett and Angela Liston's rented house in, I think, Rathfarnham. The other guests, the diary says, were 'Philip's pal Christine Clear, beautiful and lively, and Marion Kelly, who said very little but to whose hand Michael clung all day; there were also times when he was clinging on to Rosaleen [my wife] or Christine – at one stage they changed places for that purpose ...

'We had a hilarious time, reading from Dineen's dictionary and singing. We sang every song we knew from about half-past two to half-past seven. Not one song finished: everybody forgot the words. Michael kept asking Angela to play a record they'd got for Christmas, Rosemary Clooney singing "Susie Snowflake", but neither they nor any of us could operate their hi-tech CD player.

'When it was near time to go home I brought M to the loo for fear he'd fall down the stairs – he'd just fallen over the vacuum cleaner in the hallway and tumbled unhurt through the kitchen door. He said he often fell going up and coming down.

'When I went back to check he was lying on the bed in the spare bedroom. I asked was he ok and he said yes. A few minutes later I heard shouting and ran up to him. He was terrified by nightmares which afflict him all the time when he sleeps, which is rare in itself. Philip came up, slowly because of his tin leg, and we tried to soothe him.

'But the point is, he's ill beyond curing, probably the cirrhosis he once told me he had, and the mental suffering and delusions that go with this illness. Grey and wizened, he looked like some impossible animal, a cross between a pygmy shrew and a tapir, who is fated to die on the day of its birth.'

In fact he died nine months later, on 18 October, aged 58.

Philip was almost ten years younger than Michael and lived ten years longer than him. Although social construction has become a kind of Lego for the hard-of-thinking, in this instance it says something about one notable difference between them as individuals. Michael, born in 1941, was a child of war and desperation. Philip, born in 1950, was a child of the hope that followed. This shouldn't have been the case, considering his lifelong experience of illness, poverty and rejection, and yet it was in his nature to be hopeful.

In some respects he was an outsider, a green before the capital letter, an antagonist of the machine, and yet an early expert with its main machine, the computer. It would be interesting to know how many websites he set up in his lifetime – mine for one – and how much he earned from all that work: as far as I know, nothing. Offered money, he was offended. He wasn't the sort of person who gives to get, either thanks or to incur obligation.

Following his death, the *Irish Times* published, on 5 February 2018, a series of tributes from friends, colleagues, and admirers, including President Higgins. In the article the words 'generous' and 'generosity' occur fifteen times.

Amongst the contributors the novelist Anthony Glavin described Philip as 'a secular saint', but if his radical innocence was Franciscan, there was a granitic determination in his sanctity. His will was like his handshake: bone-crushingly powerful.

On reflection, it could be argued that in the novels the repression of that potential conflict in his own character, which he resolved inwardly, was too true to the life. Philip's fiction underplays his personal struggles, which were heroic. He was too modest about himself.

Another contributor to the *Irish Times* tribute was the Christine Clear mentioned above. She said, 'I never knew Philip when he was poor. I was told by him and others that he once was, but I never experienced a sense of financial foreboding with him.' Christine was much closer to Philip than I was, but I'm pretty sure I knew him for longer. We first met in the 1960s at James Liddy's house in Coolgreaney, outside Arklow, and he was then, though not yet an amputee, already a veteran of illness, precariously balanced, yet secure, unforeboding, if that's a word. Swinging on crutches taught him how to support himself physically, but how he supported himself otherwise is, at least to me, a mystery.

I don't know, for instance, how he came to own his tiny house in Arran Street East, if he did own it. But I remember the shock I felt when I saw that it had an earthen floor – the Liffey was yards away so the damp didn't have far to rise. Personally Philip was fastidious: the nearest I ever saw him come to irritation was when I touched the screen of his computer – I hadn't realised, until I learned from experience, that fingerprints can leave a permanent mark.

He could also be obdurate on obscure matters of principle: when the United States introduced facial recognition technology at passport control, in 2004, he told me he would never go to America. Such an eccentric boycott could hardly be described as self-serving, nor did it bother Uncle Sam. Philip's disobedience was civil, and his stubbornness was private. These traits couldn't be gainsaid: not going was often the way that he went.

What changed his life for good, in every sense of the word, was his election to Aosdána in 1992. Making the speech as his nominator to the General Assembly was challenging: the Bann River Trilogy of novels was still in the future, and the evidence before the court amounted to three slim volumes of verse. To use Patrick Kavanagh's phrase, I 'bet the tank on the race' by telling the truth and nothing but the truth: that Philip was a true poet, and to prove it I read a single short poem. To this day I remember the stillness that followed. It was enough. His peers recognised him.

In Philip's remaining years of unremitting toil – he was a fanatical labourer – membership of Aosdána provided him with a frugal income by way of the Cnuas: the wolf it kept from his door wouldn't have found much behind it. Unfortunately, it was necessary because the critical esteem the novels attracted wasn't accompanied by commercial success. On the current website of Picador, the publishers of *The Water Star* and *The Fisher Child*, more than three hundred authors are named under the letter 'C' – but Casey is not amongst them. To go from winning the Irish Novel of the Year Award, in 1995, to being a ghost before you die, at least in London, was a hard station.

The last months of Philip's life weren't made any easier by the Arts Council telling Aosdána, in 2017, that it was 'aware that the problems which arise for those artists who are unable to work due to accident or illness are serious. However, it cannot pay a Cnuas in these circumstances.' To be fair, the Council's scheme of sending inspectors to artists' home to check up on their output was never put into effect. Had they arrived at Arran Street and found he wasn't there, *but in hospital*, one can be sure they would have regarded his situation with compassion. On the last occasion he and I met the subject of the Cnuas wasn't raised, but that may have been because he was in the hospice in Blanchardstown.

Oddly enough, institutional cruelty had become a central concern to Philip at a mid-point of his career. Although he had no training as a historian, he set his mind to writing a history of slavery. How far he rolled the boulder up the mountain in that Sisyphean endeavour I don't know – I do know that he spent countless hours researching Irish slaves and slave-owners on the island of Montserrat in the Caribbean. One can only hope that the work has survived and will eventually be published in some form or other.

But the academic worth of what he did was incidental to doing it. Self-aware as ever, he described the slavery project as 'quixotic'. Unlike Don Quixote, he wasn't tilting at windmills; to Philip history was the pursuit of poetry by other means. He certainly wasn't a 'Knight of the Woeful Countenance', as anyone who heard the great shout of his laughter will testify. In that sense it is better to remember him as an Irish version of Cervantes' original model, the Gentleman, a word with its roots in generosity. As a lover of freedom in general and of women in particular, he was one of those rare virtuous beings described by Van Morrison as 'knights in armour intent on chivalry'.

Thomas Lynch

REGRET
i.m. Philip Casey 1950–2018

I never went the distance with you, Philip,
never booked the ticket, never flew
the red eye from Detroit to Dublin,
never paid my last respects, or showed up
for your siblings, shouldered the weight of you,
shoveled earth over you, bore that witness.
A good excuse is not a job well done:
I'd a lame dog in his own extremis,
gone from bad to worse that February.
The upstairs bedroom had become impossible.
His shoulders going, gone for months, his hips.
All milky cataracts, his blurry eyes;
a grave dug in the corner of the yard
before the frost hold of winter. I spy
your labored crossing over Grattan Bridge
from an upstairs room at the Clarence Hotel
in Wellington Quay, in Dublin 2.
After dinner with old pals, you're heading home,
surefooted in your everyday valor –
the way you made your life's hard journeys forth –
the stations of your cross and passion, borne
on crutches. Oh, dear man, you've finally become
that windfall oak, wood and bark, pain and hope,
perfected in our memories, pure metaphor.

Catherine Phil MacCarthy

LAVENDER FLOWERS

After several days' storm, I go
outside this morning and sit

by the blue mosaic table
on the patio in bright sunshine,

taste the nutty undertone of coffee,
a tingling freshness in the air.

Withered tips of lavender
inch along the garden border.

I cut each silvery grey stem
down to its green foliage.

Dozens of purple flowers stand tall,
the fragrance on my fingers

saying nothing whatsoever
about the shock of torrential rain,

and gales that tore at calm roots.
Already the first of September

and cooler, lavender blooms
as serene as ever, not knowing

what winter may bring
and whether destiny holds a future,

asking only to flourish,
exhale the essence of summer.

Terry McDonagh

PHILIP CASEY, POET AND NOVELIST VISITED HAMBURG

When I think of Philip, the word friend is the first word that springs to mind. He was a generous man who shared his table and his knowledge without reserve. Philip died on February 4th 2018 at the age of sixty-seven – much too soon. Even now, when in Dublin, I sometimes walk past what used to be his home in Arran Street East and wonder if the current occupants are aware of the impact Philip had on all who had the pleasure of his company. I don't stop and look at number 56 anymore but I still shed a silent tear.

I paid tribute to Philip in *Live Encounters* in March 2018 and much of what I write here is a repeat of that tribute. I first got to know Philip when Patrick Duffy introduced me to him and Ulrike Boskamp in Hamburg. It was 1987. Philip had been in Berlin to visit Ulrike and they were returning to Dublin via Hamburg where they were spending a few days.

This first meeting grew into a friendship that lasted until his death. In the intervening years he was to return to Hamburg a number of times. He read and facilitated creative writing workshops at The International School, where I worked. He read to rapt audiences and was a great success. He was proud to read in The Shamrock – the first Irish bar in the city – a kind of cultural enclave run by the very unusual and creative proprietor, Mike Gillen.

In 1994 we staged his one-act, two-hander play, *Cardinal*, with Guelma Lea and Barry Stevenson playing the parts – Guelma, a female security guard and Barry the Cardinal. I'm working from memory here as I no longer have the script. It's a short play, more a piece of dramatic dialogue between mismatched characters. The Cardinal, less secure, despite his high office, is eager to converse with Angela who keeps her discreet distance – but as the piece develops, she becomes closer to the Cardinal. There is little action and no resolution.

I have to smile when I think of one special, memorable moment: Philip and I went to a local Kneipe/pub for a few beers. On our way back to my flat, his prosthetic leg became somewhat detached and, instead of becoming annoyed, he burst out laughing saying, *Casey is legless*. The beer was at fault. He had lots to put up with, but he managed to be light-hearted through it all.

Hamburg was not his only port of call in north Germany. In 2015 he was invited to read at the Poetry on the Road festival in Bremen. The Belfast poet and Bremen resident, Ian Watson, who introduced Philip, talks of the warm reception his reading received – he had a quiet authority that kept his audience in awe. Philip made his presence felt and Ian became a great fan.

Sometime in 2018, I was going through a display of old yearbooks in the foyer of The International School Hamburg, when Philip's short poem, 'A Page Falls Open' – proudly displayed on the cover of one of the books – caught my eye.

A page falls open
and the reader's name
is there.
It always has been
and will be always.

On his last visit to Hamburg, Philip stayed with us for a few days. He was visiting and doing some work with Ulrike at the Arthur-Boskamp Stiftung/foundation in Hohenlockstedt, Schleswig-Holstein. I would be driving him but before we left, my wife Joanna, our son Matthew, Philip and I went round the corner to Die Kleine Konditorei for some breakfast. I mention this because Philip really enjoyed his Franzbroetchen and polished off two of them in no time. He was a man of good taste. Now, back in Ireland, I still miss my Franz.

After breakfast we set off to drive the seventy kilometres, or so, to Ulrike's Stiftung in Hohenlockstedt. I, in my arrogance, felt sure I didn't need guidance as I was certain I knew the way – but I took a wrong turn, got annoyed with myself and muttered something about a non-existent map – whereupon Philip put his hand in his pocket, took out his phone and guided us safely to our destination. We both laughed and I realised I'd a bit of catching up to do.

I visited Philip on a number of occasions on my trips to Ireland but this was our last meeting in Hamburg. He has left us, but his poem, 'Hamburg Woman's Song' remains.

HAMBURG WOMAN'S SONG

Time has gone slowly by the hour,
by the year it has gone like a day
and you and I are of a sudden old.
But behind my bright eyes, papa,

I will always be a girl of ten,
and you, a grown man of twenty
when you cheated the dreaded police
who wanted to take me away.

I was born in a time and place
to a woman I look like now,
but fear grew like mould on bread
in my mother's love for her slow girl.

I remember the sirens and cobbles,
then waking at dawn by a stream
where you left me with a countrywoman
and time went slowly by the hour.

She who was my mother
died in the Hamburg fire,
and he who was my father
never came back from the east.

My hands hardened and my bones grew long.
I trusted what I could not understand
until one morning you came up the road
and happiness changed my face.

I am a woman of Hamburg
who walked to the hungry city
side by side with my new father.
I have lived here to this day.

His ready smile and generosity will always be part of my
journey. May he rest in peace.

David McLoghlin

MISSING PHILIP

One summer afternoon in the 1990s, I was in my twenties and standing at the bar in Grogan's Castle Lounge waiting for a pint of Guinness. The front door was open to the sun. It felt continental, with the day drinkers at their tables sometimes breaking the quiet to call out to each other or to Tommy Smith, the owner. Still, I was on medium alert, attuned to the cut and thrust of the literary pub, particularly during the day, which was the time for writers and fulltime bohemians. Some had beards like 19th century Russian novelists, maybe a brown smoker's tooth: faces marked by struggle, and by smoking and drinking. Unlike them, I found it hard to locate my opinions, or my confidence.

A tall man in his thirties standing beside me introduced himself. "I'm Brian Joyce. Who are you?" He looked me up and down doubtfully: "So, I suppose you're a poet?"

"I am, yeah," I said. I had shoulder-length hair but thankfully wasn't wearing my lilac neckerchief anymore. As if baiting a trap, he asked, "Are you published?" He was thin, wearing a black leather jacket over a paisley shirt, jeans and Chelsea boots.

I was on guard, but still said: "Actually, I just got a story accepted by a new journal, *The Stinging Fly*."

"Never heard of it. Probably won't last," he said.

It was two or three o'clock and I was waiting for James Liddy. James had been my transatlantic pen pal and mentor since I'd placed in The Prudential Young Writers Competition at 16. James's life partner Jim Chapson didn't usually come on these Dublin visits: incomprehensibly, he didn't drink anymore, and preferred to stay in Wexford. James shambled in out of the sunlight with his entourage.

He was like a friendly bear with his shirt tails hanging out from a navy jumper. In a good mood, he talked about the train from Arklow, riffing in a deliberately breathy voice: "Beautiful views of the beaches. Ireland in the summer. Beach Pims! No. 2 cup is pleasure cup!" Then back to a regular register: "I used to take that train with my mother. We'd stay at the Shelbourne, bring The Pope O'Mahony to Jammet's. Jammet's!" Then the riffing might begin again.

When I said, "So, how was the walk over from Connolly?" he said, "bit of gout today, so going was slow," then, querulous: "anyway, it's *Amiens* Street. And *Kingsbridge*." He spotted Liam Brady, the ex-IRA man, at the counter, then grinned, raising his voice: "Of course, I'm a Redmondite! *Blueshirt. Latin Mass.* Pre Vatican II." Apart from Vatican II, I didn't know what he was talking about.

Tommy Smith was looking on in a clean white shirt with the sleeves rolled up, his mane of white hair matching his white five o'clock stubble. He smiled a toothy smile, taking us in, and said with a Cavan accent, "How 're you, James?" He would have a word for the older adults like Liam O'Connor, Paul Funge, Brian Arkins and Philip Casey if they were there, and a nod for the rest of us. "*Tom-my*," James would say, stretching the name like taffy. "And how are *you*?" His voice was old-world Dublin mixed with something Midwestern, quaint and humorous. "The rest of us" was me and James's various male American students, who were usually as intimidated as I was by the dizzying references flying back and forth.

The days that Philip Casey popped in, he would order a shandy or a coffee and settle himself carefully on the outskirts of the galaxy orbiting James. He never came for the full session, whereas typically I got day drunk on James-in-Dublin-days and was hungover by 6pm. Of course, I now realise that Philip was probably at work on his novels and not willing to let his concentration go up in pub smoke.

While performing, James would periodically meet Philip's eyes and nod, a shorthand I didn't understand, but presume it contained their long history. I have sometimes thought that, despite James's literary envy, there was a respect there. Philip would go on to publish with Picador, the legendary publisher, but was happy to be part of things without dominating, catching up with Liam O'Connor or the others, laughing appreciatively as James performed.

I'm sure that Philip and I talked; actually, he might have listened more than talked. I knew he was a poet, but I was in my James period, eagerly absorbing the Beat writers and post-Beats from his "non-required reading" curriculum, and I never read Philip's work. A large part of it was self-absorption. Another part was because James never said: "Philip's a great writer. You've got to read his work." Of course, the onus was on me, but I lacked agency at that age, and tended to follow a mentor's suggestions, hook, line, and sinker.

The truth is, I didn't appreciate who it was that was dipping in for an hour, two at most.

Eight years after the last time I saw him, it was a shock to recognise Philip as a character in a book, only to discover that he had died. The book was *Drinking with Men* by Rosie Schaap; the chapter title, "An American Drinker in Dublin: Grogan's Castle Lounge". In the essay, Schaap's undergraduate self meets "The Poet", a serious writer who becomes a boyfriend and then a close friend. He is kind and wise, twice her age, and wears "an unmistakable cloak of personal tragedy".

It was the winter of 2020. We had returned to Ireland after 10 years in New York, and settled in the suburbs of Cork. My wife was in the spare bedroom tweaking her lesson plan, our three-year-old daughter asleep upstairs. I finished reading, then looked Schaap up on Twitter. After quite a bit of scrolling I came across a mention of Philip. My semi-prurient thought was, "Ah, Philip's the love interest!" It passed immediately when I realised I was looking at a link to an obituary. I was hit with guilt, that he'd died in 2018 without my knowledge. There was also grief, and regret: part of it was knowing that I had missed out on Philip. I clicked over to the long *Irish Times* article where more than 20 writers weighed in, including Rosie Schaap. Even though I hadn't known him well, I recognised him in the portraits. Kindness shone from every encounter I'd had with Philip Casey.

In 2012, when my first book was about to come out, I emailed Philip and asked if I could join www.irishwriters-online.com, the directory he maintained. He quickly added my profile and was very supportive. I invited him to the launch at the Irish Writers Centre. We hadn't seen each other since the late 1990s and yet he came, by himself. While we chatted afterwards, a sea of relations came between us, swamping me with five copies of my book each, to sign. He nodded and smiled as if to say, "I understand how launches are." By the time I had a chance to look for him, he was disappearing down the stairs, leaning heavily on his crutches, and family was calling me back. Unfortunately, apart from the odd email, and with me living in New York, I didn't see him again.

*

After Schaap's essay, I tracked down *The Fabulists* and finally read something by Philip. I was amazed it was so good. It felt universal and personal, like *The South* by Colm Tóibín or James Baldwin's *Giovanni's Room*, capturing the Dublin of 1990, Ireland still suffering from the pre-boom economic recession. I enjoyed the many specifics such as, the "light steam rising off their coats" as Tess queues for her dole money at the Labour Exchange. Or the apple she buys "from the fruit seller on Aston Quay" my mind filling in a black pram, a stack of Granny Smiths on purple circular cardboard.

Apart from the city, and Mungo's visits to County Wexford, all of which is expertly painted, the characters are complex and well-rounded, particularly female characters like Tess. For example, when she brings Mungo home to her bedsit on the northside quays, the close third person has her regretting "the spots from her last period were still on the sheets". I can't remember other Irish male novelists being this matter as fact or non-prurient. *Ulysses* would have noted it, sniffing at it gloriously, but *The Fabulists* simply witnesses, from a female perspective. In fact Tess is arguably one of the best female characters by an Irish male novelist in the last forty years.

The book was published in 1994, a year before the Divorce Referendum and two years before divorce was finally signed into law. Just as he gives us a convincing female main character, Philip also captures the complexities of marital estrangement: in particular the childcare arrangement Tess comes to with her husband, Brian. Unconventional for the times, their son Arthur lives with his father. Tess collects him from school, cooks dinner and puts him to bed in the evenings. (Incidentally, I love the depiction of the shame she sees in the eyes of the men collecting their children from school in Fairview: "It wasn't her fault that he was unemployed and humbled like this in front of women." The clincher is "He was employed bringing his child home, like everyone else here"). On the other side, we have the long silent treatment of Mungo's estranged wife, Connie, after he accidentally sets the house on fire, risking the lives of their children and crippling his arm, a possible stand-in for Philip's own disability. Essentially what makes the book last is that there is neither judgement or prurience in his navigation of portrayals of extra-marital love, sex, friendship and loneliness.

As I read, I kept waiting for the bum note, the slightly *off* turn of phrase, but it never happens. He doesn't seem to put a foot wrong. The cassette Tess plays in her bedsit might make us smile but it's true to its time. "The dull heat of the gas fire" brings back the stuffy warmth of my grandmother's living room in 1980s Windy Arbour, Dundrum, and the "sulphur in the air as coal fires burned across the city" is very much the Dublin of that time. Details like Arthur "Holding his satchel in front of his, his knees bumping it forward as he walked" is true to life, and maybe young children still do it with overly-heavy school backpacks today? Certainly we still have the "steady flow of traffic" that you meet descending from Merchant's Arch to cross the Ha'Penny Bridge to the Winding Stair, the shock of the doppler effect as "a bus and a lorry passed, leaving clouds of diesel in their wake."

I immediately recognised the Dublin of *The Fabulists*, even though it wasn't my Dublin. In 1980, when I was seven, we left our housing estate in Ballinteer on the southside and moved to Brussels with my father's job – then on to Connecticut, then to Limerick. I wouldn't come back to Dublin until 1991, for college at UCD. By then the thread of Irish belonging had become complicated. In the mid-1980s, arriving early on a Christmas flight from JFK, for some reason we drove through the inner city. We were on our way to Monkstown to stay with friends as our house had been rented out for several years; which was a wound for me, having no place that was ours to come home to. I looked at wet cobblestones under low railway bridges, missing the city that was mine and not mine anymore.

In 1990, when I was in sixth year at Glenstal Abbey, I visited my sister in Dublin. I'd gone up before with friends for concerts at the RDS, and to engage in underage drinking before rugby matches at The Horse Show House pub in Ballsbridge. This time I was alone. Solitude was an important part of being a poet and bohemian, I felt, as were long hair and tacitly disowning my father's high-powered job with Guinness Peat Aviation. I drifted around behind the Central Bank. The Bad Ass Café was in business and there were some vintage clothes shops, but Temple Bar was essentially boarded up. Apart from the muffled sound of bands practicing in studios, it was quiet. The weather evoked the recession: damp, grey.

I didn't know who I was when I was with other people. I was too porous: their opinions overwhelmed me, but solitude returned me to myself, to a place where I could see clearly, and make meaning – or, connect with a meaning that was waiting to be discovered. I ducked into the secondhand bookshop by Merchant's Arch and bought a hardbacked copy of *Lessness* by Beckett. I knew that he had died recently. Buying it felt significant, even though I didn't understand his prose.

The Ha'penny Bridge drew me, the northside quays like bad teeth. There was a giant triangular set square beside The Winding Stair, holding up a house.

I sat on the top floor, like Mungo, and fell in love with the waitress who brought me coffee. A grown-up drink. Didn't de Beauvoir and Sartre drink it black on the Left Bank? The waitress wore Doc Martens. She had dark eyes, short cropped hair and a nose ring. I wrote her a poem but didn't give it to her. Without knowing it, I wanted to be waiting for someone like Tess. I wanted something *real*. Philip lived 10 minutes' walk away, though I didn't know it. It would be several years before I would meet writers. I sat and looked at the red-and-white checked tablecloth, the secondhand books, the rain pock marking the river. I was 17 and had just discovered Rilke. I looked at the river swirling past and felt in contact: with literature, the future. I felt like a blank space. I was a young poet in search of himself, looking for a story.

Billie Holliday was singing 'Detour Ahead' and amongst the music, books, posters, photos and potted plants, she felt an ease soaking into her like a drug. A few browsers and couples drank coffee by the windows.

The potted plants brings back the tall windows, the slow ambience, the secondhand book smell. I somehow see the plants as spider plants, hanging from long ropes from the ceiling, spawning or cloning replicas from their tips.

Alice Maher

ANKLE DEEP WOMAN

charcoal & chalk on calico

featured on the cover of The Water Star *(eMaker Editions)*

Eamon Maher

PHILIP CASEY'S BANN RIVER TRILOGY

In Philip Casey's Bann River Trilogy of novels, I am drawn
to his depiction of human relationships, his landscapes
and cityscapes, history and story, tradition and modernity,
which are played out, not as binaries, but as co-existing
entities that nurture each other. The Ireland described by
Casey is one with which I can identify: a society that made
the painful transition from the crushing repression
imposed by an authoritarian coalition of Church and State
to the one which elected its first female President, Mary
Robinson, in 1990.[1] In essence, Casey's trilogy traces a
Wexford family's fortunes from the 1798 rebellion up to
the dawning of the third millennium. During that time, the
clan was forced into exile and near slavery in Montserrat,
before ending up in London and then back to Ireland.
Their close identification with the southeast of Ireland is
one that constantly draws them to that particular area,
with its restorative sea and haunting mountains.

In this short essay, I will share a personal reading of the
Casey trilogy that will seek to focus on key themes and
motifs. I will follow the chronology of when the three
novels were published (which is occasionally different
from the timespan of the family's adventure), starting with
The Fabulists, which is perhaps the best-known and most
highly regarded.[2] It relates the love affair that develops
between Tess, who is separated from her husband, and
Mungo, whose marriage is under strain as a result of his
starting a fire when in a drunken state, almost resulting in
the death of his son. The relationship between these two
misfits is sustained by the stories they share with each
other about events that never took place, but are none the
less real to the narrator and listener for that fact. The
stories enable Tess and Mungo to savour vicariously the

type of escapades both would have liked to experience had life, marriage and children not intervened. Because they are unemployed, they can find time to meet up, make love and actually 'see' the city they inhabit. The following passage describes how Mungo yearns to record the view from the Ha'penny Bridge as he peers up the Liffey:

> With a camera he would have a legitimate reason (to just stand there) – a composition, perhaps, of the copper-green domes of the Four Courts and Adam and Eve's (church), with the Guinness steam house in the distance, slightly left of centre, completing the picture.[3]

Having lived for many years on Arran Street East, on the north side of the Liffey, Casey had a genuine appreciation of the architecture and moods of that particular part of Dublin, which is wonderfully rendered in the lines above. However, outside of the city, back in his rural roots, Mungo experiences an attachment to place that is unique to the area where one spends the formative years of one's life. Working on the family farm reacquaints him with the animals and soil, while also providing him with a sense of self-worth and a distraction from his guilt. When his mother dies, he gets strength from the support of the local community, who file up to him and his siblings in the church and graveyard to offer their condolences and recount their memories of the deceased. When it is revealed that Mungo has been left the farm, he knows that it is an opportunity for him and his family to start afresh. However, that also means giving up Tess, which will be a serious wrench. There are compensations, of course, such as the beauty of nature observed towards the end of a day in the countryside:

> The oak was ablaze with light. If he blinked, he could imagine it in flames, as he had once seen, he knew not where, a lone tree on fire. Now he could see it without blinking. He dared not blink; until, all too soon, the sun had gone down.[4]

This detailed description brings to mind the work of one of Casey's contemporaries, the late John McGahern. In his first novel, *The Barracks* (1963), McGahern portrays the middle-aged Elizabeth Reegan, wracked with cancer, who one morning is amazed at the splendour of a quotidian scene that she had never before fully appreciated:

> It was so beautiful when she let the blinds up first thing that, "Jesus Christ", softly was all she was able to articulate as she looked out and up the river to the woods across the lake, black with the leaves fallen except the red rust of beech trees, the withered leaves standing pale and sharp as bamboo rods at the edges of the water.[5]

I am not attempting to intimate any 'anxiety of influence' here, but rather to show that in his depiction of place, Casey shows himself to be adept in a similar manner to McGahern, in that both are wonderful painters of atmospheric landscapes that capture the feelings of their protagonists.

In spite of the guilt and disability Mungo endured as a result of the fire, and the trauma caused to Tess by an abusive husband, the two of them attempt to claw their way towards happiness. It seems unlikely they will attain this goal at the end of the novel (we later discover that Mungo and his wife broke up a number of years later) and it is only the restorative power of storytelling that offers them any real respite. The success of *The Fabulists*, in my view, is as a result of the universality of its theme of unrequited love and its sensitive probing of the existential anguish at the heart of the human condition. The writing is consistently strong and the changing point of view between the characters offers us different perspectives on the same episode. Often when a writer produces such an accomplished first novel, what comes afterwards can be a disappointment. For me, however, that is not the case with Casey and I lean to the view that the trilogy is exactly that:

three parts of the one canvass, each of which is vital to the whole.

The second volume, *The Water Star*, is set in post-war London and brings together another group of wounded characters. Hugh and his father Brendan work on various construction sites that have been established for the regeneration of the city after the Blitz. Brendan has been hardened by a difficult marriage to a woman who found no pleasure in sex, which resulted in him engaging in serious bouts of drinking and long stays in London, where he sought to earn enough money to support his wife and their only son. Fate dictates that Hugh will meet and fall in love with Elizabeth, a lively Englishwoman who is also involved with Hans, a German who lost his family in the most tragic circumstances during the war. Brendan, for his part, ends up marrying Sarah, who was forced to leave Ireland after becoming pregnant outside of wedlock. Occasionally she regrets the fact that she and her boyfriend Tom had not been strong enough to face down the opprobrium of the local community after the news of her pregnancy became public knowledge. She admits that although she was thirty-three and he twenty-eight at the time of her pregnancy, 'they had been too young to stand their ground against class and custom.'[6] The Ireland of that time was not one that tolerated what it viewed as sexual promiscuity, which necessitated Sarah's move to London. Tom sent money for his daughter's birthday every year, but the couple never saw each other again after she left for London.

The pull of the land is very pronounced in *The Water Star*. On one occasion, Brendan explains to Deirdre, Sarah's daughter, that the mountain in front of his house in Ireland, known as 'Croghan Kinsella', is an essential part of his identity: 'A man, and a woman for that matter, must know the name and history of the field he walks on, or he's nothing.'[7] This sentence is a memorable summation of the

Irish fascination with the land, that visceral attachment to place that is a strong feature of the work of so many contemporaries of Casey, particularly John McGahern, as we have seen. While their relationships are undoubtedly a source of joy to Brendan and Hugh, they also bring their crosses. When Hugh's son dies in a tragic accident, Elizabeth enters a deep depression which lasts a long time. When she finally emerges from it, she conceives and gives birth to another son, Dan, but she never regains the vigour and joy that characterised her personality before the tragedy. Brendan remarks at an early point that Sarah drinks to excess and the two of them spend a lot of time trying to find comfort in a bottle. Towards the end of his life, Brendan says to his son that he wants to be buried in Ireland:

> Croghan is our home. If they'd let me, I'd be buried on the mountain. But as long as I don't have to travel too far, I don't mind ... Maybe I should've gone back. I've often thought that. But then my life is here.[8]

How many Irish people of Brendan's generation had to face up to the reality that years spent away from Ireland resulted in their never being able to return to what they left behind? Brendan's last words to Hugh, 'The mountain, the mountain is our home',[9] express a yearning for the landscape that moulded him. When Hugh revisits the family home after burying his father, he can see that time has moved on and that the past can never be restored: 'A crucifix hung over the bed, and an oleograph of the Virgin, pointing at her bleeding heart, hung on the side wall.'[10] These religious symbols point to a different era, one where religion was the dominant force in people's lives, and it is clear that there can be no turning back of the clock – at this point, Hugh has no real time for religion, but that will change.

The Fisher Child introduces us to Dan, Hugh's second son, a London architect who is in a happy marriage to Kate and their two children before she gives birth to a black daughter, Meg. This strange occurrence is not the result of Kate having been impregnated by a black man, but rather because one of his ancestors, Hugh Byrne, started a family in Montserrat with a native African woman and the strain remained in the genes of their son, who was born white, although his sisters were black. The crisis occasioned by the shock of Meg's skin colour results in Dan making a trip to Ireland, where he hopes to get his head around what has happened. He stays with Hugh and begins to reflect on what life would have been like had the family never left Ireland. When his father announces he is going to Mass, Dan remarks that he didn't know Hugh was religious, which elicits the retort: 'Ah, just in my own way. The ancestors and all that stuff.' Dan finds that a bit Japanese, but his father does not agree: 'The Japanese for cars and Walkmans! My religion is my own.'[11] It is interesting the way traditional practices can often take hold as one gets older. Hugh undoubtedly finds a certain degree of peace in Ireland and religion gives him comfort, a sense of belonging. However, he realises that he left the area too young and, as his father remarked several times, 'you have to walk a place to know it properly.'[12] Hugh Byrne had discovered in Montserrat that a person faces the same challenges no matter where they find themselves:

> The trouble with the world, he mused, was that every place was local, a small parish where men with small hearts could crunch their neighbours into the dust and think themselves big men for it. He had come a long way to learn that.[13]

The last novel of the trilogy is one which emphasises the importance of place in coming to an understanding of self. Dan wonders if he truly loves Kate if he cannot trust her and accept Meg as his own. In Ireland, he is forced to see himself as he is: 'The moor was too damn desolate without the softening effect of Annagh and Croghan. Too much a damn reflection of his soul, if he had one.'[14] In the end, he returns to London and will try to resume his life with Kate and the children. It will not be easy to convince Kate to forgive him for doubting her, but towards the end of the trilogy, one has the impression that everything might work out:

> Meg woke, gurgling to herself, and he picked her up. She seemed to look at him from a great depth, unsettling him. If he'd believed in God, he would have prayed then to be granted some understanding, but all he could do was look hopelessly at this mysterious child. He rocked her in his arms, and she seemed content with that.[15]

Any father who has held his daughter in his arms will know just how special that bond is. A baby is a miraculous thing and Dan's love for 'this mysterious child' seems to be forthcoming. In the end, it is Meg who may well resolve the impasse between her parents.

The Bann River trilogy is an impressive literary achievement and it explains why Casey's death in 2018 brought forth a host of tributes from his fellow Irish writers. He deserves all the accolades he received, and more besides, for presenting such an insightful vision of existence, which oscillates between joy and pain, hope and despair, love and hate. In an interview in *Live Encounters*, the online literary magazine, Casey explained his compulsion to write: 'In a nutshell I write because I have to and I don't really want to do anything else.' Thankfully he chose to sculpt words rather than to take up any other profession: everyone who reads his work reaps the benefits of his wonderful skill as a wordsmith.

When I think of Casey, the early work of his fellow Wexfordman Colm Tóibín, especially *The Heather Blazing* (1992) and *The Blackwater Lightship* (1999), immediately springs to mind, but also novels like Patrick Kavanagh's *Tarry Flynn* (1948), Dermot Healy's *A Goat's Song* (1994), and the entire *oeuvre* of the aforementioned McGahern, all of whom had a wonderful facility to make of one place an everywhere, to give each individual life a universal significance. But most importantly, Casey stands out as a highly talented writer in his own right, someone whose *oeuvre* will continue to draw new readers long after other more successful authors have been forgotten. That is no small legacy.

NOTES

1   At the end of *The Fabulists*, both Tess and Mungo believe that the President is waving at them from the passing cavalcade just after her election.

2   Eamonn Wall's essay 'Climbing the Winding Stair: Philip Casey's *The Fabulists*', published in *Berfrois*, an online journal on 15 March 2022, provides a sensitive reading of this novel.

3   Philip Casey, *The Fabulists* (Dublin: Lilliput Press, 1994), p. 17.

4   *Ibid*, p. 142.

5   John McGahern, *The Barracks* (London: Faber and Faber, 1963), p. 170.

6   Philip Casey, *The Water Star* (London: Picador, 1999), p. 56.

7   *Ibid*, p. 203.

8   *Ibid*, p. 417.

9   *Ibid*, p. 418.

10 *Ibid*, p. 430.

11 Philip Casey, *The Fisher Child* (Dublin: eMaker Editions, 2015), p. 196. Originally published by Picador in 2001.

12 *Ibid*, p. 197.

13 *Ibid*, p. 133.

14 *Ibid*, p. 221.

15 *Ibid*, p. 256.

THIS IS NOT A LOVE SONG. NO, THIS IS NOT A LOVE SONG.

I am sitting in Philip's little house in Dublin just off Ormond Quay, so close to the Liffey, as he swings around on one leg with a full pot, hopping and lurching from counter to table without spilling a drop. We often drank our tea surrounded by overflowing bookshelves that seemed like an extension of his mind.

This is not a love song. No, this is not a love song. It is not an academic paper either. I thought of writing a formal essay analysing a poem Philip gave to me. A poem that I kept with me and never forgot, about the love of one artist for another. It's also about the failure of his poem to convey Frida's depth and passion in a new work of homage. But I couldn't do that with this poem he had given me. Instead, I will rudely gatecrash the poem Philip wrote in honour of Frida Kahlo and provide some scattering of thoughts. The poem is called 'Waking To The Plain'. Philip gave it to me on a piece of paper himself because we used to spend a lot of time talking about Frida Kahlo. I sat upstairs on the bus and unfolded it and read and reread it. Subsequently, I taught this poem in my writing classes as a prompt, to show them an example of a poem about a hero you have never met. To show them that a poem could fail and the failure could become a crucial part of the poem.

When I met Philip first at Mary O'Donnell's book launch, he was on crutches and his trouser leg was pinned up. Yet he bravely descended the steep stairs in La Cave wine bar undaunted. I didn't know exactly who he was but I knew he was the person in the room I wanted to talk to. He never talked about himself or his own achievements; he was always intensely interested in other people. And he had a way about him, lit from within, and he could give you full attention and make you feel special. Everyone loved Philip because he radiated this kindness and attention. And he brought these qualities to the page every time, which makes his poetry so munificent, so expansive, so full of love and humility.

In the room Philip and I come and go, talking of Frida Kahlo.

As we sat sharing a bottle of wine in La Cave, I told him I'd been to Mexico City many times. He immediately asked me if I'd been to Casa Azul.

'Every time,' I said.

And that's where it started. Philip and I are talking about Frida. We used to joke that we knew her before she became a household name! Though Frida Kahlo had always been beloved in her own country, in the few decades after her death she took over the world. Partly, because there was a new feminist art history movement that acknowledged women painters. Philip wrote this poem in 1990, in that moment before she became a brand, a brand that risked rendering her a commodity, which often eclipsed her art.

> Here I painted myself, Frida Kahlo, from a mirror-image. I am thirty seven years old, and it is the month of July, nineteen forty-seven. In Coyoacán, Mexico, the place where I was born.

So starts the poem Philip wrote about Kahlo. It is fitting that he gives the beginning over to her voice. Philip was always generously amplifying other writers. Despite the fact that he was under-appreciated in his lifetime and never got the attention he deserved, he harboured no resentments for other writers' successes. However, he wasn't averse to my evil ranting. I'm nowhere near as magnanimous. I could see a glimmer of amusement in his eye as I trash talked some of our contemporaries purely out of disgruntled jealousy.

I myself had stumbled on Kahlo by literally following some signposts. After saving up my tips working as a waitress in San Francisco, I was floating around Mexico as a 22 year old. I set out to see Trotsky's house in Coyoacan. After I had inspected the bullet holes in Trotsky's wall and looked into his empty chicken coop, I noticed there were signs to Frida's house right outside Trotsky's door. So I stumbled curiously in happy ignorance around the block and in through the massive blue walls of Casa Azul. Like so many, I was captivated by her painted torso casts, her kitchen, and her mirror on the bed, so she could paint while lying for months on her back. I noted her obsessional love with a man who looked like a giant bullfrog.

Philip approached Frida as a disabled artist like himself, one who knew pain. The poem he shared was two poems in one; his original attempt of a poem describing her paintings, and then the battle within the poem of how he could only fail at this. Both strands of this poem curl around each other, and like the mysterious Fibonacci shell they lay out the mysteries of the universe that we are grasping to unravel and reveal.

> I tried to understand you through the self-portraits you
> began when the collision of a bus and tram changed your
> life as time slowed down.

Here he states that he merely tried, not that he ever actually understood. And we know right away that he will fail. He is letting us know this too. Her pain moves him because he knows that other country of chronic pain. He senses a kinship in this knowledge.

> They chronicle the trials of your body's broken column;
> your love affair through two marriages with Rivera; the
> miscarriages; your passion compressed into a high tension
> and expression.

The poem then focuses on *The Tree of Hope*, where there are two Fridas on the canvas. She often painted herself in double as a recurring motif. One of the Fridas is scrunched, inert, and naked on a hospital gurney with a bleeding back wound, and the other Frida, by contrast, is resplendent in her red dress, holding her back brace as if to discard it. Strangely, the injured broken faceless Frida is in the sun, and the surviving strong Frida is in the dark. We discussed this. We had no answers. Philip knew it was not the artist's job to provide answers or even ask questions. It is the artist's job to drag us into the profound depths of life where we can make our own inquiries, and develop our own justifications for staying alive. Philip's poem looks intently at her work, but respectfully does not strive to explain her.

> I must have known it was impossible, but blinded
> by what I thought was love – and it was, by some measure
> – I made draft after draft, losing my way through your
> subtle world of guise and fantasy, through
> what is at once concealed and revealed.

Suddenly Philip breaks the rhythm of the poem and despairs that it is an impossibility to write this one. It's too deep for him. After all, he himself had lain on hospital beds. He too had to wake up from an operation without his leg. We never talked about that. In a way he never positioned himself as a disabled artist, and he saw that in Frida too. The pain was part of her work, the suffering, the hacking away of a limb, but never the definitive part. There were always two Fridas, and two Philips. The maimed physical ones and the ones that were made whole by art.

Though this poem is impossible for him to write he won't stop struggling, because he knows that there is some mystery there, something he has to get to the centre of. Some slow story pilgrimage into a spiral shell. Philip breaks into the poem as the struggling poet to allow the failure of one artist to get through to the depth of another over time, space, nationality, gender, circumstances. But really the mystery is love, the kind of rare numinous love when you connect irrevocably with another artist solely through the power of their work. Philip loves Frida, and so meets her time and time again on the paper, yet fails to write the poem he wants, that even measures up. Time and time again he stumbles from the dark side of the canvas to the light where his words meet her image, and his words have to flounder.

> *The Tree of Hope* was my prime enigma:

> Dressed in her red Tehuana costume,
> she is Kahlo the desert queen,
> reigning over her butchered flesh and bone
> that lies defeated on a surgical trolly –
> where the moon is mistress beyond the orange sun.

> The moon, Frida, and that old orange the sun, that your
> childhood teacher held in one hand – a candle in the other
> – to explain the solar system. Darkness and Light. And the
> fissured desert that stretches to the distant, eternal
> mountains is the desert that encroaches when hope is
> ruined too often. Isn't that so? The images return to haunt,
> and I repeat the attempt to write them out:

Philip is asking questions, 'isn't that so?' as if he needs reassurance, or maybe telling her he knows the fissures in the background desert are scars, gaping wounds of pain that both he and Frida know so well. This poem is a product of repeated attempts, and many drafts and failures. He is haunted by the work he can't complete.

> Bound in plastercast, she paints in
> the hair on her lip from a mirror-image,
> rapt in search of the meaning of what
> she is doing again, and again, and again.

Then he swings us around out of the poem and tells a story, as Philip was a storyteller at the core. He tells of the first meeting, how he was introduced by an artist in

Germany to Frida Kahlo's work, and that very night how a spirit came. Again the notion of haunting:

> After dinner one night, an artist told me about you. The house we were staying in was old and later I sensed a ghost in my room. I think it was a part of myself, long forgotten.

At first I thought it could be Frida's ghosts coming to him. But he doesn't say this. Just as she often worked in doubles, here is his double, another Philip approaching, a lost part of himself. He stops there, no more to say. We don't get to know the other Philip. What part had he forgotten of himself that now came back, now that he knows Frida once existed? Philip moves away from his own ghost to explain how this artist followed up and sent him images of her portraits that launched his infatuation.

> A few months later a letter arrived from a friend:

> A bulging letter, postmarked Berlin.
> I read the excited hand, unfolded
> the black and white copies: Kahlo.

> So began the obsession. Spring passed into summer, and one evening I ambled down Kilmainham Lane, admiring the elderflowers, the peace of this *rus-in-urbe* broken only by guard-dogs and the rhythmic clack of my crutches. Then an odd thing happened:

> A red car stops, a puff of dust
> rising before the tyres,
> and a Mexican woman asks for directions.
> Later, in a bar, I asked her about Kahlo,
> who, she insists, painted with colours
> which don't exist in Europe.

Here the poem introduces another character, a random encounter. Not an artist but someone from Mexico in Dublin. And in these lines I see something very Irish, very Philip. A tourist stops and asks for directions, and Philip, like any Irish person worth their salt, must have talked to her and found out where she was from. Before you know it they are in a bar. This makes me smile. Of course he is gleaning information about his Frida. Then the poem moves back into the descriptions of other paintings.

> The burnt siennas of your Mexican earth, Frida; your
> yellows at once pouring out sickness and fear, sun and joy;
> your dark blues occupying both distance and tenderness.
> Dark green, you said, was the colour of bad news and good
> business. There is bad news and good business in your
> *Henry Ford Hospital, 1932.*

> In the Henry Ford Hospital, Detroit,
> Frida has lain in her own blood
> since 1936,
> her miscarried foetus spirited above her
> like an African fetish – her pelvis, her tear,
> the hopes of her famished love – so much debris.

> Its foreground is green, and the spiritual drama of your
> miscarriage is played out against a backdrop of Henry
> Ford's factories delivering Baby Fords. It took me a while
> to see humour where previously I could recognise only
> suffering. Now I'm glad to know it was typical, like your
> parrot who drank beer and tequila and croaked: *I'll never
> get over this hangover!*

Those words echo within me, 'it took me a while to see humour where previously I could recognise only suffering.' I hear them in his mellow Wexford accent. Philip was a funny person, and he loved to laugh, great big booming laughs with his hands over his crutches and his head thrown back. And I relished making him laugh. We'd talk about the wreckage of the world as it drifted unmoored, and rottingly fell apart like Rimbaud's drunken boat. And then we'd find something funny in the flotsam. So there would always be the light side and the dark side to our meetings.

> This is a quote from the story of your work and life by
> Hayden Herrera [...] A friend sent it from New York, while
> another gave me reproductions I had never seen.

Suddenly the poem talks about many of his friends sending him things about Frida. I myself used to pick up little boxes in Mexico City painted with her words, or decoupage items with Frida's paintings, Mexican folk craft. I brought him back the Mexican money with her face on it. He would always treat these little things with delight. I suppose I wanted him to know that, even if they were kitsch, they were chosen for him, that I loved him too. That he was irreplaceable for me as an artist and a friend. That his work moved me, that I would fail too if I tried to write a poem for him. I am failing now.

> It was then I realised that all my drafts were false. I was
> writing about myself.

Philip has an epiphany. We return to the ghost that first came to him when he was told of Frida, his first encounter. It was himself, a forgotten part. The reaching out to her across worlds couldn't work; it was false. It's not often a poet reveals the collapse of the poem within the poem. The sham awkwardness. The defeat. The deficiency of words to match a life, or even a painting. And he feels that this was a 'harassment' and unfair of him to try to get to her beyond her art.

> I have harassed you for significance for too long. You are
> what you have left behind and the only way to discover
> what you mean to me is to forget all I know of you, and
> think of whatever comes to mind. Yet, as if I were in love
> with you, you can appear anywhere.

The poem is an admission of his great love, and how she keeps coming back to him replete with significance. One artist to another. One sufferer to another who suffers. One being who knows pain and only pain and who laughed at it and used the hurt to make great art.

Something as formerly innocent as a cloud or landscape or as utilised as a polluting bus, can recall you as if you were seated in them, a mirror before you, your brush in hand.

So many correspondences where nothing is strictly itself might unbalance a mind. How many women limp through a crowd? Might they have light moustaches, or eyebrows joined like batwings?

They, the correspondences, are sane because you are unique, like a giant lake from which rivers flow through the thoughts and emotions of those who need you.

Frida is sending Philip messages, correspondences, in other women limping, or traces of her unique face. I remember when I first saw her images in the Casa Azul and I was shocked that she had kept her unibrow and moustache. I'd never seen a woman allow herself to do this. I thought we all had to prune and starve and pluck and shave and please men by pretending we were so different from them, so inhuman that they could never be us, never have to be us, or understand us.

One time upstairs in Bewley's Cafe, Philip and I were reading at a Cáca Milís event. He could not walk up the steep steps to the stage so Helena Mulkerns, the writer and MC, reverently brought the mic to him. He remained at his table and read to the audience with the lamp beside him. The audience swung around to surround him. The room was hushed and we were mesmerised because another Philip appeared, the poet, who was absolutely solemn about the sacredness of the words under the lamp. The act itself, the oldest ancient practice of how we let each other know that we honour our flawed broken lives, that we love everyone, even those who take everything, because it's all we have and that's what poetry is about, this love. Otherwise we could just do something solid and sensible with our lives, and not wrestle with these perplexing double selves and crafty ghosts.

I savour that moment because Philip was not always appreciated as an artist. Publishers were not publishing his books in the end. He was not young or in fashion. I knew that hurt. He had given everything he had to the craft and it felt as if it wasn't wanted. The seeds he scattered were drying on the surface of the soil. Many of his contemporaries soared to fame, but he was an artist's artist and he wanted more. I did too. We were kindred in ambition and failure. His close friend Marion told me when she sat with him as he was dying that she asked him very close to the end where he was going and he said 'I don't know'. That was an honest answer. But he went because he had to, because his body wouldn't host him anymore, into the dark twisted path of the curling shell, back to the beginning, or to nothing, which might be where it all began.

It was a longish life. He was still only in his 60s when he died, and he yearned for more than he got. I know that. Maybe Frida did too, in her lifetime she was often just known as Diego's wife. Artists can't know where their work goes, or how it pulsates after they have become dust; the ink scratches on the page, the coloured oil strokes on canvas, they have their own heartbeat that's not our fragile mortal heart.

This is not a love song. This is not an academic essay. I don't know what this is. It is my own failure to convey how much he meant to me. How his work is more than our consolation, it lives and breathes, it haunts. Never again will Philip make me tea so precariously in his kitchen in Arran Street East. But I see Philip, my wise friend, my sometimes mentor, my fellow seeker scribbler, my kindred bearer of disappointments. I see him in the last lines of this poem, the poem that failed him, the poem that became two poems, another appearing like a ghost inside the poem, the light poem, the dark poem, the triumphant, resplendent poem, and the broken backed poem that turns away in agony.

Perhaps the Fibonacci mystery shell is meant to protect us, the winding way back home, a home with no pain, no disappointment, no more poems falling apart on the page. No more waking up with limbs gone. No more rejections. No more forgetting parts of ourselves. And Philip Casey must have gone where he sent Frida Kahlo in this strange wonderful poem, because it was himself he was writing about all along:

> She floats, asleep
> in canopied rest, rooted
> high over the earth –
> her vigilant companion
> a Day of the Dead skeleton
> decked in dynamite and flowers.
> She has journeyed a long way,
> and no one can follow
> into the shell
> of all she has yearned for.
>
> – 'Waking To The Plain', Philip Casey, 1990

Paula Meehan

LETTER TO PHILIP CASEY FROM AGIOS KIRIKOS

Your doppelganger ganging down the gangway
today; along the pier a halt, a stutter in the flow,
your dark blue raincoat, your stick pegging memory
to my line. A wind out of the west — a zephyr —
loosed from a god's wind-bag ruffles your locks, tender
    wind
that warms the earth for spring blossoming, that kindles,
that feeds the funeral pyre, that births the ocean's white
    horses

in myth. But it's not you this morning. Passing the sad café.
'Make it new,' you'd say. 'Fuck Pound, what could he know,'
I'd say, 'of our lives. Make it old again, make it starry,
volcanic, magmatic, under so much pressure
it be obsidian; let forest be coal, be diamond.'
Adamant, in the way of young poets with our spindles,
our symbols, our blessings, our riddles, our curses,

our yarns. I am by memory gutted as if a bird of prey
had swooped into the quotidian, a shadow
on the mountain, and plucked apart my reverie.
Once, near the end, you gave me a peacock's feather;
radiant in firelight like some longed for twinned
dharma brother, stranded in East Arran Street, candles
and burning birch casting bronzed light on your verses.

≈

I thought the spring would never come.
And though spring will never come for you again
You are in all my springs

And we rove out
Our manuscripts clutched
In childish hands

How innocent we were and wise
Beyond our years
How much we trusted

How much we feared
How lightly we carried
The weight of our years

≈

I see you now, son of water,
son of river water, your white river
the Bann, flowing past Hollyfort, lustred mirror
to your childhood; in her shimmer, a glimmer
of all the great rivers ahead, their charmed daughters,
and you, bright maker, their beloved singer.

In dream you come to me overbrimming with health,
strong in limb, your eyes blazing with truth;
you are planting fruit trees, the loam a fine tilth;
as you dig, an orchard grows, flowers in your wake: wealth,
you tell me, is what we hold in common – it be kin, it be kith.

You were our polestar, our guiding light, a beacon
in the obscurity and loneliness of our worst season;
you held the line, you did not weaken;
you shine eternal now, lucid in some angelic region.

How often we spoke of destiny, the spinning wheel of fate:
sean nós, fado, rembetika, the blues — the weight
of suffering a covenant, a sacred obligation to create.

Come the moon in solemn metric patterned from deep
    trance;
come the stars, the wheeling stars, to join our gallant dance.

Come the weathers, old friend, of those days, that in your
    light
                             we live and die and love.

Helena Mulkerns

PHILIP BY LAMPLIGHT

For a long time, Philip Casey was a mysterious, online *Wizard of Oz* figure for me. Since I lived abroad for most of my adult life, I encountered him first only as the spirit pulling the strings behind an amazing website that compiled and uploaded a broad-reaching body of information on Irish writers. I initially presumed it was run by an arts organisation, or the English department of some university. When I realised it was basically one person, who was generous enough to single-handedly create an entire site for free that promoted other people, I was intrigued. Before I even knew he was a poet and scribe himself, I saw him as a pioneer who, enticed by the starry potential of the burgeoning internet, took innovative action in the days before the behemoths polluted the virtual spaces.

Meeting Philip in real life reflected the quiet, steady power of his fiction and the eloquence of his poetry, but did not by any means diminish his *Oz* quality. When the conversation begun on the web eventually became a friendship in the ordinary world, I remember being struck by a certain magical aspect to him. Soft-spoken, a little androgynous; I confess that the word "elfin" came to mind. But that could change in a flash, too. While he would discuss, gentle and curious, any theory or tale, he'd then all of a sudden let out a Falstaffian guffaw or wicked riposte that blasted away any ethereal adjectives with a resounding Wexfordian clout.

While the marvels of nascent digital publishing technology took up much of our conversations, Philip, who had long been involved in live arts events in his native Wexford, had a deep love of performance. He had long participated in a range of events from the early live readings in French's pub on Gorey's main street in the 1970s to the legendary Gorey Arts Festival and many, many further live events and literary festivals as his work became known. During a conversation we had about the merits of blending music or other arts with straightforward literary readings, Philip expressed interest in a theatrical venture I was running at the time at the Wexford Arts Centre.

'The Cáca Milis Cabaret' was inspired by my grandfather's stint as Master of Ceremonies at the weekly rebel entertainment in Frongoch prison camp of yesteryear. Adapting the necessarily eclectic lineup of the original, Cáca Milis presented contemporary original work by emerging and established writers, musicians, dancers, clowns, film makers, artists and comedians in a sort of old music hall style evening of the arts. The centre's director Elizabeth Whyte originally proposed it as "recession-busting" theatre in the mid-noughties. The Arts Council championed it there for several years, but its new Dublin-based events operated on a bare shoestring. Philip, unfazed by this and seeing it as a tongue-in-cheek version of "people's cabaret", offered to read at our "D-Day Cabaret" in Bewley's Café Theatre, 6 June 2013.

I was delighted, but concerned. While Philip had long used crutches, he underplayed any impairment his mobility issues posed with a dignity that skilfully hid the reality of his health. It went without saying at the time that this subject was not up for discussion. True to form, there was no question about getting to the venue for the gig; he just showed up.

The event was memorable. Philip emerged from Bewley's Victorian lift with his colourful crutches, sat into the crowd and enjoyed the Blitz sirens that we kicked off with in darkness. Josh Johnston and I sang songs from 1944. The mic was brought to Philip's table to facilitate his reading of several poems – one set in Germany – that went down perfectly in the cabaret ambience. He was followed (much to his delight) by the very lovely Miss Azaria Starfire, who danced a cheeky parasol-and-feathers number. Patrick Chapman read a story, Morgan MacIntyre (now of Saint Sister), delivered original songs, and the evening played out with Truly Divine singing Dietrich.

During the break, Philip found out that an audience member sitting near him was an Irishman who had flown as a pilot in the Battle of Britain. To mark this extraordinary fact, he called for a fresh 1944 song for the pilot, and there was a round of applause to thank him for his service, almost seventy years earlier. Philip was sold on the cabaret.

Throughout that year, he was also self-training in innovative new open-source software that expanded his technical talents in the area of indie publishing. He set up eMaker Editions, and would successfully re-issue his Bann River trilogy, for which he had retrieved his rights from Picador. It was through these works, initially encountered on his own website, that I found the poetry and fiction that marks him out as an exceptional artist.

His debut novel, *The Fabulists*, was one of the first books I'd read that nailed the grim desolation of Dublin in the late 1980s, which prompted so many of us to take flight pretty much as soon as the Leaving Cert was over. Its tale of yearning and escape paints two flawed people trapped in a brutal world. But the author is kind to them. Their sensuality is rendered graceful despite the squalor. In his second novel, the single eponymous moment when a lonely twenty-two-year-old glimpses a star from the rubble of a post-conflict wasteland shows how Philip's poetry and compassion weave seamlessly into his fiction. Today, the book's theme of exile and displacement resonates more strongly than ever. Since they were at that time out of print, it was very exciting to know they would soon be available again.

For Philip, it was especially important that the new digital printing and distribution methods allowed books to be published not *just* as ebooks (we both agreed ebooks were not proper books), but as real, high-quality paperbacks available to order internationally online, with ebooks an option to the hard copies. Ever the instigator, it was Philip who persuaded me to put the work of the writers and poets who had performed at the cabaret into an anthology, *Red Lamp Black Piano*.

By Christmas 2014, with *The Water Star* and *The Fisher Child* now live for sale too, Philip was up for another Cabaret. We'd moved to a new performance space – Arthurs – on Thomas Street. Clicking through its website, Philip was taken by the unusual 18th century building, which had retained just the right amount of its former Georgian splendour to distinguish it as a venue. Its carved stone fireplace reflected in darkly-silvered mirrors that hung over the staircase, with corniced high ceilings doming the stage. *Put me down*, he confirmed. *I'll read from one of the new editions*.

It wasn't until the day of the event that I found out in horror that there was, in fact, no lift from which Philip could emerge, as before. The venue had not yet been adapted for disability access. I cursed my lack of awareness and basic manners. Philip was so good at making everyone around him feel comfortable, he almost never mentioned health issues, or if he did, it would be briefly. He approached life like a veritable Buddhist warrior. I was terrified he might be offended if I suggested we call off the reading, but felt I had to risk it, and so phoned him at home.

Philip assured me this was not an issue. He was scheduled to perform, and he'd be there without fail. A little later, as we were setting up the café tables, Philip appeared at the top of the stairs. He had simply come early, before the arrival of any other performers or punters, and quietly tackled the sweep of stairs at his own pace, without fanfare. He accepted a strong cup of tea and a scone and settled just in front of the stage, in the glow of our signature "little red lamp" on the piano.

Also on the bill that night was fellow author Mary O'Donnell, already a Cáca Milis favourite, who had performed in Wexford the previous summer. Russian tribal bellydancer Nadia Gativa jingled yuletide sequins, The Late David Turpin gave a hybrid multimedia/live performance and Carol Keogh sang from her new album. For some classic Christmas, glam-nós chanteuse Caitríona O'Leary performed, among others, 'The Wexford Carol'. Burlesque diva Lola Grey delivered a rambunctious Dickensian parody, and there were mince pies and Christmas ditties at the piano and spot prizes, then flaming Christmas pud lit by the barman, turned showman for the occasion. The performance ran late ...

Just a little later again Philip, in flying form, made his way back down the stairs without fuss, just good cheer and tinsel-topped crutches. This time he was joined by a jolly crew of friends and fellow performers who accompanied him down to the street and into the Christmas midnight clear.

There are so many ways to remember Philip Casey, he was a good friend and an inspiration to a lot of people. Polymath, poet, jester, novelist, forger of the new, rebel against adversity, not to mention MC of his very own one-man literary salon in Arran Street, Dublin's smallest arts centre. Of all of these, one is my favourite: Philip by lamplight – cabaret hound.

Philip, 2013, by Barry Delaney

Cáca Milis Cabaret, 2013, by Michael Stamp

Aidan Murphy

SNAPSHOTS OF A FRIEND

I first became acquainted with the work of Philip Casey in the late 1970s when our poems began to appear in the same broadsheets, newspapers and journals: *Cyphers*, *Stony Thursday Book*, *crackedlookingglass*, *The Cork Review*, 'New Irish Writing' edited by David Marcus. In those days the platforms for publishing poetry were scarce so it was inevitable that young poets became familiar with the names of contemporaries.

We first met in person early in the 1980s shortly after Philip's debut collection, *Those Distant Summers*, was published when he stayed overnight with me in London on his way to mainland Europe. My first impression was of a soulful, boyish man with an affable disposition. He had a passionate affinity with European literature, art, theatre and music – which is clearly evidenced in the work he produced for years after. That particular evening I remember being delighted by his knowledge of the writings of Jack Spicer, an American poet who performed his work live in the bars of San Francisco and had died at the age of 40 in 1965. I thought that nobody else in the world had heard of Spicer, but Philip was surprisingly erudite on the subject.

In the spring of 1987 I moved from London to Dublin, renting a room on the North Circular Road. At the same time Philip was lodging in the home of the artist Evanna O'Boyle in Inchicore, and I became a frequent visitor there throughout that summer and autumn. They were memorable times during which we cemented a lasting friendship. Languid, lively afternoons and evenings of good conversation, plenty of laughter punctuated by the odd glass or two of vino. We were all poor as church mice. Philip had a room upstairs which consisted of a bed and books ... books ... books. It had a monastic quality which was Philip's style: the bare basics, no luxuries. The world of the mind and the joy of being alive were luxury enough. He wrote about that room, or should I say painted with words, in his poem, 'Inchicore, Early Autumn, 1986'.

Philip and I shared the same publisher, Raven Arts Press, which later morphed into New Island. Raven was a dynamic flagship in its heyday, steered by the capable hands of Dermot Bolger. Open to new ideas, new voices, it enticed many fine writers. I was privileged to assist in the editing of *The Year of the Knife*, Philip's selected poems published by Raven in 1990 — a volume I would recommend for anyone interested in his poetry. Over the following twenty years our paths crossed on many occasions by chance or design. At exhibition openings in the Royal Hospital, Kilmainham; at poetry readings and book launches throughout the city. He would always be there with a warm embrace and good humour.

Our mutual friend, the poet Matthew Sweeney, paid regular visits to Dublin on literary business or stopovers on his way to family in Donegal or to see his daughter in Belfast. By then Philip had found a modest house on Arran Street East and it was usually there that we three met. It was heartening to see that Philip experienced some solace and security there. An odd, unlikely trio we made as we haunted the bars on both banks of the Liffey and the back of the Four Courts. At that time, if I remember rightly, Philip was having serious problems with his prosthetic leg. It was outmoded and an improper fit, abrading the raw skin and making it so difficult to walk on that he would sweat profusely even over short distances, which was the reason to confine our meetings to the vicinity of his home. Others might have raged with bitterness and blame having been dealt a poor hand. Not Philip. Never in public. He was stoical and realistic in dealing with his pain and had no truck with the Disney consolations of the Catholic Church.

I have fond memories of those rare liquid lunches. They were often fiery but never problematic. They were mini-workshops as we showed each other finished poems or work in progress. We spoke of personal problems, present situations, literary gossip and of course the latest books, movies and music albums. Sometimes our sessions descended into hilarity and bawdiness – boys will be boys and grown men will be silly. Philip had a droll wit and a refreshing earthiness about him. He had a hearty booming laugh that belied his gentle speaking voice.

The last time I saw Matthew was at Philip's funeral. He was gravely ill then and would be gone not long after. The poetry stays with us. Philip tackled tough themes – pain, loss, death, social injustice, oppression by church and state – but he approached all subjects with genuine compassion and a muscular tenderness. His style was robustly crafted yet rich with lyricism and dreamlike imagery, retaining the wonder of a child. In my mind I can easily see him as that kid in the old tale who saw the naked truth behind the Emperor's fake finery.

Eiléan Ní Chuilleanáin

THE CONVERSATION

… and when I die
will I be transformed into a thought
travelling at the speed of light?
— Philip Casey

The shiver travelling up the cat's backbone
when something flutters in the garden,
a shiver in water moving under thin ice –
it's the nearest thing to the live
thrill in the air that is Philip now.
It's a flutter that stops before finishing
since it needn't be entire to give
his singular greeting.   To reach it again, though,
you have to pause. The map is crumpled up,
East Arran Street hidden between the folds
where nobody searches now. I want a likeness
taken somewhere on his travels
in plain daylight by a journeyman's hand. I can see
the years of his life that were taken,
the years of work too, but the years
he gave away to the big conversation
afford his best presence, a voice
that speaks, that knows its right to a hearing:
And this is how we spend our days.

It echoes in the corridor
Where they queued on plastic chairs.

A field full of words,
a field that Cadmus planted,
a voice that speaks about them all.

They have almost run out of chairs
but the doctor still sits in her dim
packed office, reaching still for forms to sign
to certify the condition has not changed,
as the traffic slows on the quays of the city.

Padhraig Nolan

COAST
i.m. Philip Casey

It is early, Mister Casey,
in the day, in the life
of a young writer somewhere
down the country,
realising her world can be
rebuilt in words.

It's early, Philip,
in the working day
and I am thankful
that it is not me out there
blaring horns along the N11.

I wish those cross-horned
motorists a breath
of the calm and deftness
with which you opened
your page like a sacrament
when first we met.

Serenity which certain rooms
in Dublin will always recall,
fogged as they now are
with your absence;
the charged brush
passing quietly.

LEGLESS WITH MIRTH

My friendship with Philip taught me much. First and foremost, he valued writing as a powerful means of expression, but never underestimated the difficulty of using the written word to good effect. He made it clear that this priority would be a conditional dictum in whatever way we engaged with him by quoting Thomas Mann in his email signature: 'A writer is someone for whom writing is more difficult than it is for other people'.

As a doctor, I was constantly impressed by his stoicism in the face of daunting suffering and disability. He shrugged off the consequences of illness with humour and a philosophical acceptance that there were many worse than he. Recounting to me once, with customary tolerance, the results of one of the many investigations he had to undergo, he wrote: *I had the CT scan on Tuesday. It went fine but the trace fluid irritated my bladder and had me urinating all night. When I mentioned 'trace fluid' on the phone to my mother, who was a nurse in London during the war, she misheard me. 'Did you say you had to drink Jeyes Fluid?!'*

He helped me in many ways, not least in setting up my website, as he did unselfishly for so many others: *I've just finished designing a website for disabled people – designing websites is my hobby, and I love it, but I think of it as akin to reading comics.*

Philip joined me in a campaign to ban landmines, and no one understood better than he the awful pain of losing a limb:

> Mao Sopheap was orphaned by a landmine. Then, when she was 16, she stepped on one herself – her left leg was blown apart and had to be amputated. During an interview she cried: 'That mine has given me a future of tears until the end of my life.'

But Philip never complained and often made light of his disability; one evening after a few glasses of wine in a pub in town, he headed off for his quay-side abode, as he put it, "legless with mirth".

Which leads me to his sense of humour and mischief. *The Funks of the Screw*, which he founded with Marion Kelly and Ronan Sheehan, were:

> dedicated to the remembering of the brilliant and the bold of Ireland's past luminaries, often misunderstood or forgotten. With an emphasis on conversation, commentary and friendship, the Funks will seek to emulate the conviviality of their 18th century exemplars, *The Monks of the Screw*, who *mingled mirth with wisdom, and gave to political philosophy the charm of eloquence.*

I helped Philip as best I could with his independent publishing ventures. He had become fascinated by one of Nevill Johnson's paintings, 'Dark Head', which he found 'haunting', and eventually it graced the cover of his novel *The Fisher Child*. I proofread *The Book of Rights: The Story of Irish Slavery and Servitude*, as it was first called, and urged him to submit it to publishers from whom he received mixed reaction. *The tiny feedback I'm getting from agents suggests that yes, they like the writing very much, but think it isn't commercial. I think they're wrong, but then I'm not an agent, and wouldn't dream of telling them they were wrong!* It behoves all of us who knew him to make sure that this important work sees the light of day.

At our last meeting in his home on Arran Street East on 30 December 2017, I was put in mind of the sentiments expressed by Christopher Hitchens in *Mortality*, the cruel paradox of intelligent minds grappling with the inevitability of death – their death, and their hopeless reliance on orthodox medicine and its practitioners (of which on this occasion I was sadly counted as one), mixed with frustration, amounting to anger at our impotence to offer explanation, comfort and even unorthodox therapies in the face of the impending inevitability. I left Philip saddened by my feeble utterance of useless platitudes and my inability, as a doctor, to bring solace to a dying friend. And then a poem epitomising Philip's generosity of spirit eased my sense of hopelessness:

I drag myself on decrepit crutches along
the lightless quays and almost fall over
a supine man. 'Help me,' he croaks,
and despite the frost in my bones,
yet again I drag him to his feet. 'Thank you,'
he says for the thousandth time, 'you'll prosper for it.'
'I wonder,' I say, as he makes his way without me.
'No, I'm certain that I doubt it.'

Jean O'Brien

BALANCE
i.m. Philip Casey

Knowing where your body is in space
is not as simple as it sounds.

We plant our feet down where
we first find ourselves on earth.

It takes time to stand and more
again to put one foot in front

of the other, to walk, to ambulate,
to step. We maintain our equilibrium

by finding the parameters of our bodies,
often with the help of another body

to indicate where we start and end,
a hold, a hug. We begin and finish

where another's flesh strokes us
connects us to ourselves.

Our birth makes us live inside
our own skin without breaking.

The air around us vibrates
with our presence, as we strive

to find our measure,
create harmony, sing an Aria

we can only try to live within

as *ordinary mortals*

step
      by
            step.

Mary O'Donnell

PASSION FLOWER ON ARRAN STREET EAST
Remembering Philip Casey

I note the new front door, its red sleekness.
Within, bookshelves and stacks, dingy sofa
and happy purpose, all laptops and research.
We laugh softly as he prepares coffee,
scooped in hillocks on the bent spoon,
then honey and ginger cakes. The table
is a smooth plateau, a heat-ringed surface.
He opens a page of Lowell. I read.

Later, he speaks of Ulrike, all gleam
and generosity. Near the window,
the cupulate mauve of a passion flower
blooms in the yard of this city quarter.
In scant sunshine, purple petals
make mischief on tropical mornings.

Michael O'Loughlin

THROUGH A GLASS BRIGHTLY:
THE POETRY OF PHILIP CASEY

Though Philip later became better known as a novelist, poetry was always at the heart of his practice as a writer. His first published book was a collection of poetry, *Those Distant Summers*, published by Raven Arts Press in 1980, in what now seems to those of us who knew Philip then and attended the launch of the book in Gorey, a very distant summer indeed. There was a sense of opening and promise, as well as clear accomplishment, of the first resolute step on what would be a long career.

Though it was a first collection, Philip's voice was already recognisable and filled out, as it celebrated his childhood and youth in that beautiful corner of the world:

To the North rose Annagh Hill
the colour of raspberry juice,
and blueberry-blue Croghan Kinsella.

The voice was also honed by his sojourn in Spain, which for many Irish poets before us, but also his and my generations, was something of a Swiss finishing school, where we went to learn a new emotional palette, and to be baptised in the eternal blue of the Mediterranean. There are other terrestrial voyages, and voyages through the works of others: but most importantly, through the dark and bright stretches of the human heart, *sol y sombra*. Much of Philip is already there. In an early poem like 'The Chamartin-Barcelona Termino Express', we see his interest in, and sympathy for the lives and pain of others, something which would lead into his novels.

In the small hours, as the women sleep,
a man gives me *jamón* and wine.

> He's eager to talk of his sons in Europe,
> and religious wars in Ireland.

This empathy with his fellow humans is also evident in works like 'Liffey Bridge', from his second collection, *After Thunder*, published in 1985:

> A drunken beggar falls asleep,
> wine seeping from wind-broken lips.
> Sealed into his swollen being,
> he sleeps on a cold bridge and dies.
> ... A closed box
> of closed thoughts: the proud dead cock
> that never crowed.

In what is one of his finest poems, from the same collection, 'An Indian Dreams of the River', he gives a voice to a Native American recalling her rape and her husband's murder at the hands of European invaders: "how they broke my husband, bone by white bone." It is an act of reparation, which never loses its integrity as a poem, and remains one of his finest achievements in poetry.

That physical pain, and the strange synergy of nothingness and light it brings with it, is never far away in Philip's poetry, as in his life. It is no wonder that one of his later works details his obsession and identification with Frida Kahlo, and his attempts to get inside the skin of the Mexican artist whose works throbs with the intensity of physical pain: "her butchered flesh and bone/that lies defeated on a surgical trolly." In the end he gives up, but still continues to encounter her as a kind of muse in unexpected places: "Something as formerly innocent as a cloud or landscape or as utilised as a polluting bus." The poem ends with lines which could be applied equally well to himself:

> She has journeyed a long way,
> and no one can follow

into the shell
of all she has yearned for.

In his next collection, *The Year of the Knife*, published in 1991, we can see many of the themes of the novels already being rehearsed. There are the vignettes of bohemian Dublin in the 1980s and 1990s, the lost world of damp flats and counting coins to buy bread, familiar from *The Fabulists*, now hard for the current generation of Irish novelists and poets to imagine. But also the theme of the Irish and other nationalities in exile, the long secret history of the emigrant, and the ones who stayed at home, which he would explore in novels like *The Water Star*. But here they are already, in poems like 'The Irish Wait':

In a rough port in its cold Welsh night
the Irish wait, exhausted, to board
a ship for home.

This dual existence of the typical Irish migrant of the 1950s and 1960s, the Irish, like Philip himself, randomly born in either Ireland or Britain, who spent their childhoods shuttling back and forth between identities, finds its voice in Philip's poetry and prose, a voice usually heard not in the official literature of our times, but more often in "a grieved, ill-remembered, rebel song."

Another aspect which his poetry shares with the novels is his interest in the countryside he grew up in, and a foreshadowing of his later passionate ecological concerns. In one of his most trenchant poems, 'Through A Glass Brightly', there is an almost Kavanaghesque vision of rural life. Apart from the constant beauty of the landscape, of tree and flowers, he is also aware, as he always is, of the private pain of its inhabitants, the almost invisible people, and the importance and universality of the parochial. The poem describes a walk through the landscape, to visit neighbours:

the old couple who had lost prosperity
through his drinking, set teas and cakes
and we listened to the affairs of the realm.

His later ecological concerns were already present. As he walks through the rural landscape, he notices how:

Once on the road, a young grove
was to our left – later our father
reclaimed it for grass with his spade.

The landscape is not innocent, nor are the people who work it. Like his own family, they need to make a living from it. Though he would spend much of his life in the city of Dublin, he never lost that countryman's insight.

In the title poem, however, Philip explores another unreported world, the almost endless nights of hospitals and pain, in which he somehow manages to find a redemptive, hard-won light. As he says in the opening lines:

This voice speaks because it must
when it overflows with endless night,
the jaws strained tighter than a Norman bow.

It's hard not to see a reference here to his Wexford roots, the county where the Norman invader Strongbow first set foot on Irish soil. But it also recalls the rabbinical instruction: "Speak not because you have something to say – speak because you cannot remain silent." And behind many of the poems in this book and in his later work, we feel the pressure of silence, the will to articulate his particular experience.

This voice speaks because it can.
In the sleepless reich of phantom pain,
it struggles to name the nameless.

The struggle to name the nameless would become the force behind may of his later poems, as his struggles with physical disability veered into areas rarely designated, perhaps most perfectly expressed in the poem 'And So It Continues', worth quoting in full:

> Beyond the headstones in the graveyard
> there is a special plot for limbs.
> Severed legs and arms
> mingle promiscuously in death,
> if they missed their chances in life.
> The hand of someone's husband
> rests on the leg of someone's wife.

If nothing else, these lines could justify his poetic project. And like many of his poems, a sly wit is never far away.

Like many poets, from Yeats to Derek Mahon, in his later years Philip could not resist tinkering with his earlier poems when he reprinted them in his *Tried and Sentenced: Selected Poems*, in 2014. The reader's experience of this is a matter of personal taste. For someone who grew up reading his earlier poems, it can be a disconcerting experience to read a familiar poem like 'The Chamartin-Barcelona Termino Express' (1977) in a radically different form, like meeting an old friend you haven't seen for many decades. But it's dangerous to make a value judgement on such personal foundations. Maybe we need to leave it to future generations to weigh them up? What can be said now is that the revisions are a paring down, a stripping back to the bones of the poem.

The last poem in the book is in fact an early poem, where already Philip had abjured the cosiness of iambic pentameters, and instead set down short phrases and individual words: Waiting. Fatalistic. Curious. Stoic. Human. If he was trying to write his own epitaph, he succeeded.

As a young man in the early 1980s, I set off to live in Barcelona. Philip told me to look up his friend José, who had a humble cafe in the *barrio* of Barceloneta. When I sat down to Philip's favourite dish of fried eggs and *garabanzos* I mentioned his name. The proprietor immediately hugged me and told me what a dear friend Philip was.

The impression of reading Philip's poems is often like that. It's like having a conversation with a dear friend, full of wisdom and compassion, but one who has seen the dark side of things also, and has a sometimes hard, astringent, clear-eyed view of reality, which he won't hesitate to share with you. The kind of friend we all need. There is no doubt that Philip's poetic *ouevre* will stand beside his prose works, as a unique legacy of a difficult life lived with grace and joy.

Nessa O'Mahony

DO NOT ASK
in memory of Philip Casey, 4 February 2018

We didn't plan for it,
but these past days
we've stalked death,
been stalked by it
as we wandered streets,
looked up at domes,
tried to remember the past
without googling it.

Skulls everywhere:
on market stalls,
behind glass in the ritz
of Burlington Arcade,
bells tolling each footfall.

Then the pink room
where Keats spotted red,
signed his death warrant
in a four-poster bed.

And here, now, returned
to our borrowed bed
in the shade of St Paul's,
we take our beat
from the chimes,
till the phone beeps
with the news.

You'd have seen the joke;
were always the first
to try out new technology,
match it to old words.

Another bell:
and I know
for whom it tolled,
old friend.

Mary O'Malley

Fastness

Beautiful morning. Praise the kestrel's spiral,
the sparrowhawk's aerial runway
low over the roof, the light stilling the room.
You have been gone awhile. The house
always knows you will be back.
It will demand only a fire, a clean,
the lick of paint long promised.
Unjudging, kind, its modest twists and turns
are tuned to joy and disappointment.
Here we are again, it says. Here we are.

Paul O'Reilly

WINDFALL OAK

On a Friday evening in 2004, it was my job to collect our
fiction workshop facilitator, Philip Casey, from the train
station in Enniscorthy. Having also been given the task of
booking him a B&B, in our first sequence of
correspondence Philip had asked for a downstairs
bedroom. I didn't know why, nor had I the courage to ask,
but then I realised why when I saw him alight from the
train on his crutch and walk slowly down the platform. It's
hard to recall the exact chat we had, but I welcomed him
and spoke of the rebellious, heroic and often tragic history
of our beautiful town – of which, of course, he was already
well aware. We crossed the Slaney on the Séamus Rafter
Bridge and drove to his B&B midway up Summerhill, the
only one I could find with a downstairs bedroom.

The next day, the series of workshops hosted by Launch
Pad – a creative writing initiative and open mic forum that
had been started in Murphy-Flood's Marconi Room by a
group of like-minded enthusiasts interested in all things
artistic, and of course a wee tipple – took place in St
Aidan's Primary School, where our then chairman Andy
Doyle taught. Philip took fiction, Eamonn Wall poetry, and
Mike Hanrahan and Leslie Dowdall took songwriting.
That night a majestic open mic was held in the more
spacious IFA Centre on Mill Park Road, where facilitators
and students performed, bands played, the theatre group
acted out scenes, many drinks were had in between, and
renowned local writers like Peter (Cursed) Murphy,
Mogue Doyle and Martin Codd read from their works in
progress. It was a tremendous success, and relationships
both began and blossomed that weekend that would – and
will – continue for the rest of our lives.

Then, in 2005, the first edition of *The Scaldy Detail* – originally conceived as an anthology broadsheet inspired by the earlier publication, *The Gorey Detail*, which Philip was also involved with – was published by Launch Pad. Eamonn Wall edited, and Niall Wall and I did much of the correspondence and early design. In it was 'The Windfall Oak' by Philip, and it brought me to tears as I read. I would later tell him the impact of his words, by the timing of them arriving in my inbox as much as anything else. Because, earlier that year, my father – a man I had thought absolutely invincible – had unexpectedly died.

Philip's next visit to Enniscorthy was in June 2007, for the launch of another *Scaldy Detail*. For this edition, he kindly submitted the first scene from his screenplay, *Long After I'm Gone*, set in the aftermath of the 1798 Battle of Vinegar Hill, based on his novel *The Fisher Child*. This time, having prepared a bed in a downstairs room, he stayed in our house in Urrin Valley, just outside the town. Our first son was not yet a year old, and Philip was such an easy, undemanding, educating and entertaining guest. Over red wine and homemade lasagne, he spoke of books, the old days in Gorey, the value of anthologies like ours to new writers. As talk moved on to the responsibilities of parenthood, both then and later in life, with our son sitting on my wife's lap watching in wonder as us adults laughed and toasted, we were enthralled at Philip's story that one of the first books he'd ever been given to read as a frustrated teenager, by a perhaps more liberal adult than those closer to him, was *In Praise of Older Women* by Stephen Vizinczey. It is a measure of how easy we had all become in each other's company to talk so freely about such a book, one neither my wife nor I were aware of at that time. But, needless to say, in the weeks after, a copy was ordered and still resides in our home beside a treasured, signed copy of *Dialogue in Fading Light*, a gift as thanks for his accommodation.

Over the following years we kept in touch, Philip always so encouraging. He kindly read my early fiction, and helped steer me along the way. Whenever I asked if he would accept some payment for his time, even a voucher, anything, he declined, asking only that I show the same interest in emerging writers when my time came. This I have always strived to do. It was so typical of Philip's outlook and hope that the kindness he showed us writers would somehow gather momentum, continue, spread and never stop.

It was early 2015 and my own debut collection of short stories was to be published later that year. Philip showed an interest in it and agreed to give some notes. And should he be so inclined, or dare I say impressed, perhaps he would give an endorsement. From his correspondence, it was clear he was lacking energy, suffering, but still he persisted and over a number of weeks his spot-on notes trickled into my inbox. Here, it became even more evident of how diplomatic Philip could be when issues arose, his attention so attuned and passionate about the impact of a scene I was trying to nail down:

> No doubt you'd have spotted this yourself in your final review, but ... I find this very much problematic, especially if read, as it inevitably will be, by a family who has experienced suicide of one of their children or siblings. The last suicide wake and funeral I was at ... still haunts me, and suicide is so complex and mysterious I think it's incumbent upon us not to make emphatic statements. So, as I've no doubt you recognise, you have an enormous responsibility to get this story right. I make a simple suggestion in the notes below. Less is more, I would say.

Always the mentor, the guiding light, when I had pushed the boat out too far, as a writer to this day I remember that my reader may also be a victim (just like my fictional one), as well my responsibility to *get it right*. It has been one of the most lasting lessons I've ever learned, and it came from a man of integrity and experience. Even when the honesty was going to be tough, it was still wrapped in words that were as generous and encouraging as possible ...

> I hope, after all your work, that this critique so late in the day won't make you weary, but better a supporter like me than a vicious critic.

I had the pleasure of hand-delivering a copy of my book to Philip at his home in Dublin where I was greeted like a king. But, sadly, the next time I got to visit was when invited by his family to take a book to remember him by. Another old mentor of mine, Jim Maguire, once said that sometimes he picked up books in shops and bought them, not knowing why at the time, not having any real intention of reading them. But, eventually, that gut feeling reason becomes clear. And while it took me until Covid to read Philip's copy of *The Clown* by Heinrich Böll, I would soon go on to draft a play where an actor walks on stage in a clown's outfit.

But, today, most of all, any time I think of Philip, especially now after his passing, it isn't long before I am brought back again to his own intensely lived-in words and worlds. And not only because of the timing of them arriving in my inbox, but by the emotional bond I still have with them.

> On that childhood isle find a windfall oak
> and hollow it to his measurements.

The death of my father in 2005 had a profound effect on me, and not just his passing, but the time I've spent since, missing him, wondering what he would say in certain situations, would he have given his blessing to works I'd go on to write, produce, record. Over the days following, the weeks, months and years, I have often thought what kind of grandfather he'd have been, wished he had been afforded the opportunity for even just a short time. His passing would teach me many things; even in death he would be a mentor. I had never thought about it previously, but it quickly registered that I was now next in line, and the picking of a coffin was an experience I never had before. To this day Philip's poem brings me back to that tightly packed room: its smells of varnish, polish; my hands on shining woods of many shades; the feel of the insides; the pressure of selecting his final bed.

Make sure he goes in his casual clothes.

My mother picked out what he felt most comfortable in when alive, yet what both of them deemed presentable when entertaining guests.

No fancy lining, just wood and bark,
the rough-cut halves secured with rope.

A man of simple needs, he loved home-cooked food, to fix things rather than throw them away, to choose a Saturday night TV wine based on taste, not price or fashion.

Seal it if you must with wax,
then form a circle around this fallen tree
to celebrate his loves and laughs,
the route of his ink, his pain, his hopes –
and do so in well-made song and verse.

A man of some renown, his songs and poems were well-regarded. His tenor voice even more so as were his duets with my mother. And as for social gatherings …

Quench thirst with your favoured drink
and join if you will in a wild ceilidh.

They loved to live life to the full. From weekend sessions of song and music in the many pubs around Wexford to the countless places fleadhs brought them to.

Then plant the sapling in the earth.

But everything comes to an end, eventually. However, from death something new can spring to those left behind, often when it's most unexpected. Not a mere inheritance, but something more devastating and wonderful and fulfilling, from just a memory, a photograph, a reading of their words that when seen in this new light can breed new meaning in your life.

Much of what I have said about my father, I can say about Philip Casey. He would also become a mentor to me, a distant yet immense father-like figure, and even still – in death – he has many things to teach. From his wonderful legacy there are phrases that still evoke emotion, that still provoke, often bringing us back again to a difficult experience or painful place we've also gone to. While it is a most admirable talent of a courageous writer – one who lived with so much pain – to not flinch in times of sadness or heartbreak, so too is it a talent and a kindness to remind us that we are not alone in these feelings. With Philip there is still a purity in his message, whether it was spoken and remembered or written down, and a promise that – with patience, and reading, with good friends and some good faith in all that is precious on this earth that makes it worth living in – the dark clouds can lift and those terrible thoughts that come at times can be replaced with a simple will to be there for others. In the same way he was, for me, for us. In the same way he shall always be, in spirit. I leave the final words to Philip, who perhaps gave us a clue as to the source of his generosity in his poem *Mourning*:

> The phone rings. Somebody wants me to do
> something for them, and I do it for you.

Rosie Schaap

My Dinners with Philip

More than twenty years of friendship, and the first image of Philip Casey that comes to my mind is this: we're at dinner with our friend Marion Kelly, a decade ago or more, at W.J. Kavanagh's in Talbot Street – a restaurant that closed its doors some time ago. The dining room is full and humming, aglow in gentle lamplight, and everyone – every diner, every server, every cook – is terrifically beautiful, all spirits are buoyant. We sit at a round table, nestled in comfortable old wooden chairs, and we might have ordered almost everything on the menu.

We taste from each other's plates – steak and fish and spuds and veg and pudding – and toast with glasses of wine and whiskey whenever the feeling strikes. We are overjoyed with the food and the drink and the ambience and ourselves – and, more than anything, with the fine company we have made of each other.

Our feast ends, but the bliss lingers: we're still laughing as we charge south towards the quays, Philip flying through city streets, even cobbled ones, on his crutches, in that balletic way of his, powered by the superhuman strength of his upper body. From time to time, Marion and I link arms with him, maybe to slow him down – who would want to speed up such a night? Who would want it to end? And Philip makes a courtly joke: *A woman at each arm. Lucky me!* Lucky us.

And after the meal, the drinks, the flying walk, I have this thought, a silly one but the truth: no one takes pleasure in pleasure quite as Philip does. In a morsel of meat. A sip of whiskey. Blue cheese swooshed across a cracker. A good tale (especially when he was the teller and cracked himself up mid-story – the enormity of that laughter). A beautiful line in a poem. The best word in the right place.

In that associative way that memory works, one remembered dinner leads into another. Our first: in 1991, the year Philip and I met (in Grogan's), the year I made my first trip to Ireland. It's my last night in Dublin before I go home to New York. I don't want to go. We eat heaping plates of handmade pasta at a (long-defunct) restaurant that might have been ahead of its time; who, back then, would ever have imagined the day would come when one could choose between sushi or pho in Capel Street, just around the corner from Philip's Arran Street East home? We splashed out on a good bottle – Barolo, likely – to share.

That summer Philip hadn't dined out much, so he savoured every bite of tagliatelle, and all the cheerful chatter at surrounding tables, too – not too loud, but alive. No lulls in our conversation, either, ever, and I sensed then what I'd come to know for certain later: a brilliant writer, sure, and also the world's greatest dining companion.

Fancy (*ahem*, 'deconstructed') fish and chips at that hotel in Temple Bar.

Special occasion dinners upstairs at Fallon & Byrne.

Sushi in Capel Street!

Our first, but not last, meal together at L. Mulligan Grocer in Stoneybatter: we sit at the warm old wooden bar and fall hard for the place, the staff, the engagingly written menus crafted from old books.

Every time you come to Dublin, he says as we stroll toward Smithfield, *you introduce me to some fabulous place I didn't know existed.*

I visited Dublin as often as I could afford, and a visit without going out to dinner with Philip – well, that was no visit at all. Restaurant intel was the least I could do.

(His generosity: One had to be sneaky if one wished to treat Philip. A whispered word to a waiter on the way outside for a smoke. A credit card pressed into a maître d's palm when Philip was in the loo).

Our last dinner out: Mulligan, again. This time, with our friends Nicole and Sara. Another joyful night – much food, much wine, much laughter. It must have been summer, or a warm night anyway, because in a photo from that meal I'm wearing a sleeveless dress, something I doubt I'd ever done in a Dublin restaurant before. I am hoisting one of those tulip-shaped whiskey glasses – a bit of Powers John Lane, which Philip and I had tried on that first night at Mulligan's, and of which he and I approved deeply. I am smiling widely, something I never do. My face shines, probably from sweat, but it looks like only happiness. I am showing off a new tattoo: a portrait of William Blake on my right shoulder. Here's Blake now:

How do you know but ev'ry *Bird* that cuts the airy way, Is an immense world of delight, clos'd by your *senses five*?

Whose senses were less closed – more open – than Philip's?

Smell. Sight. Touch. Hearing. Taste. Sense.

Sensuality. Sensibility. Sensitivity.

Intimately sensitive to suffering, and injustice, to the cruelties of the past and the present, he also was the rare one who *knew* that a single flying bird is immense world of delight. And that a dinner out with friends was its own world of pleasure, replete.

I flew to Dublin for his funeral – a decision I had to make quickly, leaving no time to arrange a place to stay. Aware of my dilemma and of my love for Philip, Seáneen Sullivan, an owner of L. Mulligan Grocer, invited me to stay in the flat above the restaurant, and I availed of her kindness.

The night of the funeral, I lay in bed and closed my eyes and listened for Philip downstairs – for his laughter, his uncontainable, head-thrown-back, full-body laughter. And I could still hear it. I still can.

Gerard Smyth

A LAST VISIT TO ARRAN STREET
in memory of Philip Casey

We come for souvenirs,
for the ink-black pages of Philip's books.
Each of us to choose where to leave a gap,
disturb the ordered alphabet
of scribes and scribblers, unknown and familiar.

An August Sunday
not like the last time I was here
when snow was on the way
and among the things he said
there was no mention of misfortune or distress

or any kind of torment of the spirit or the flesh.
The river at his door was coming to full tide,
we sat and talked and reminisced
as if any minute the spinning world
might stop spinning.

And now on this last visit to Number Fifty-Six
we see his empty chair, notice what's missing
from this nest on Arran Street:
the fits of laughter, the parlour discourse.
But there he is, in the frame, like Solomon grinning.

Colm Tóibín

O'GORMAN'S LEAP

Philip Casey sits by the Aga in the kitchen.
All over the house, courtesy of those huge speakers
Van Morrison blares.

Outside, there is the village. But for a few hours
Other places loom, not least Parnassus.
Also, French's pub in Gorey.

No one really knows why O'Gorman, the doctor's son,
Leaped from the upstairs study window,
Through the summer greenery.

Half a century has passed: his landing in the flower bed
Still has a tangled sound, and he must have groaned.
By which time

Philip Casey was standing at the door of the study
Wondering what all the fuss was about, shaking
His head and smiling

Before turning away to be alone for a moment,
Not bothered by much, least of all by the recent leap
Of O'Gorman, the doctor's son.

Drucilla Wall

BUTTERFLY AND STONE

Any walk through Philip Casey's poetry offers reflections both interior and philosophical, as well as exterior and observational, exploring his experiences with aesthetic elan and poetic precision of language. The warmth and humanity of Philip himself weaves through the work. I have never known a writer more caring, curious and open to others' lives and works. An afternoon in his company filled me with admiration for his adventurous nature in artistic projects he set for himself, and the life challenges he met with courage and grace.

Philip Casey's sitting room at the front of his Dublin home, a modest brick row house near the old fruit and vegetable market, was lined with books, his desk and sofa nearly covered in files, loose pages of notes and research materials. The odd teacup, emptied and forgotten, dotted the scene. Photographs and art filled the few spaces among the bookcases. This place of comfort, thought and work made me welcome. A short hallway led back to his kitchen where we could have tea at the small table nestled near one wall. All one could need for cooking and household convenience was carefully organised. He laughed easily and made me feel that I, too, could do great things.

Among the Wexford poems, 'Through a Glass Brightly', from *Those Distant Summers*, captures a country walk layered, as if with oil paint glazes, the vibrant details of lives, gardens, farms and light, distinctive and often overlooked. "The first few steps would/be past yew trees and/rows of raspberry bushes … The day would be fine,/ probably a Sunday in late June." The poem continues recreating a grove, wild strawberries, a milk stand, lilacs under telegraph wires. The poignancy of memory reveals that the "rushy fields" are gone like so much else, but the mind's eye sees "the fallow field where he and his brothers would play hurling on summer evenings." A more Wexford scene I cannot think of. And the distant "Annagh Hill, the/colour of raspberry juice,/and the mountain of the gold/legends, Croghan, Kinsella." Further remembered observations list a cottage, dogs barking, hens blocking the path and an intimate childhood scene in the calm, protective woman's kitchen where "they would set tea and cakes/and he would be a prince,/listening to the affairs of the realm". The sense of loss in this poem, as in many others by Casey, is balanced by a sense of the eternal present in which nothing is ever lost and all is happening now, as it ever was.

In sharp contrast to the golden light of memory, Casey just as often depicts a harsh, even gruesome, observed reality. In two of his Dublin poems in *After Thunder* the physicality of death can almost reach the reader's nose. 'Liffey Bridge' offers, "A drunken beggar falls asleep,/ wine seeping from windbroken lips,/sealed into his swollen being,/he sleeps on a cold bridge and dies ... The proud dead cock/that never crowed." And, in 'Everpresent by the Grand Canal' from the same volume, "Strewn corpses of unwanted pups/bloat in a dull tract of water./... Wars fought within mad wars,/... in the livid street;/the black smoke of bombs, the entombed/noise of hearts breaking are ever present." The bending of time in Casey's poetry reminds us that change may be constant, but also repeats itself like a refrain we cannot escape.

The abstract poems are driven more by the play of ideas than concrete imagery, although his use of imagery is as powerful as ever. One of my favourites straddles a zen-like fence between philosophy and actuality. 'The Warm Stone', from *Dialogue in Fading Light:* "Beneath the starlit sky/after the heat of the day,/we are talking quietly/of beliefs/which matter to us ... For a precious interval/we have found the ease/of hard-won simplicity.//... a butterfly, like a hand/conducting a silent *adagio*,/comes to land on a stone,/then is still as the stone." The statement about simplicity could not be more eloquently highlighted than by the stillness of butterfly and stone, both living beings, as radically different from each other as they are from human consciousness.

In 'Making Space' from *The Year of the Knife*, the speaker muses about the scientific principle of the Conservation of Energy. In a darkly humorous way, the speaker wonders: "does it apply to me,/and when I die/will I be transformed into a thought/travelling at the speed of light?/... whose molecules keep your bedroom lit./I will burn for you all night." Perhaps that is a fine lover's consolation. If one must die and leave this world of laws of physics, at least one could burn all night as a lamp.

Philip Casey shows great range as a poet, of which these few examples give a glimpse. This final poem I have selected shows the depth, as well as the breadth, of his work. Casey suffered lengthy hospital stays as a child, and overcame health issues and chronic pain through his whole life. The poem, 'White Horse', from *The Year of the Knife*, is one of his most powerful. Keenly observed details, combined with spiritual and philosophical engagement, as well as artistic skill, make it shine like a surgeon's knife. It cuts the reader deeply along its path.

In Irish traditional culture, the white horse can be associated with death, the mythical creature that transports one to Tír na nÓg, land of eternal youth. The title image rings the first note of grief for the poem, one of Casey's more lengthy pieces at fifty-two lines: "Nights in a hospital cot:/beyond its bars/a great toy horse/that a child's breath/could rock.//A crab blindly crawls/through blood,/to devour marrow/until the bone is hollow.//The radium machine hums ... aimed at rampant cells,/burning them and the flesh ... and at every turn,/one of the children/will live beyond reason,/to sift long for a sign/of why one might survive/and another must die." Late in the poem the horse has a rider: "The pale Queen has passed,/astride her white horse./... lets fall one/from her purse of death/into the endeavour of rebirth.//Watch over the sleeping children,/white horse. White horse, rock."

The fullness of the poem includes hospital imagery, conflicted in being both healing and cold. The tortuous question with no answer – why must innocent children suffer in a world created by a loving God (if one accepts that belief) is embedded in the poem. The poem offers no answer – that would cheapen the lives depicted – but rather drops into our minds the presence of an ancient rider on her white horse, one who gives no answers and no mercy. Those who survive will live haunted by those who did not. And yet, the poem has a completeness of form in employing the horse as a frame that creates comfort, if only on the page.

I will always remember fondly the afternoons of tea in Philip's kitchen. I will always carry immense respect for his poetry in its beauty and power. He is able to write with an inward gaze that also invites all readers to see how the inward connects with the outward world. Reading Philip Casey is to walk with him through all terrains of life, from golden fields to hospital beds, from the eternal present to the unknowable questions of the ages.

Eamonn Wall

A New Body Every Day
Philip Casey and Disability

Once when I was speaking to Philip Casey, I described the Irish Writers Centre on Parnell Square in Dublin as a good venue for a literary event. At that time the venue did not have an elevator. Philip answered, *Not if you are disabled.* Though this was not the result he had intended, I felt like an idiot for saying something so careless and stupid.

As an infant, Philip was diagnosed with cancer of the groin. At the Royal Northern Hospital in London he received intensive radium treatments that, while curing the cancer, resulted in a lifetime of complications and interventions. In the years since Philip passed away, I have sought to lessen some of my ignorance by exploring what is now known as Disability Studies.

I never thought for one second about querying Philip about being disabled because I thought that it would not be right. We spoke as one writer to another, and as friends. I asked him about his poems, fiction, history and his digital media projects, and he responded by asking me about mine. I knew that he suffered greatly, and sometimes he mentioned it; however, his push was always in another direction, and it was to find out about me and what was going on in my life. Deflection? Of course. Should I have asked him about disability? Maybe. Would I have been uneasy doing this? Hell, yes. Philip and I were always comfortable together, and I would never have wished to disturb such a great friendship.

Here is what William Bradley has written of his experience with radium:

> As we all know, radiation can be very effective at curing cancers, but also effective at causing cancers as well. For this reason doctors are careful about pointing the radiation

beam directly and specifically at the malignant mass. To help calibrate their radiation machine they draw targets on the patient's body – for me those targets were tiny blue dots that go down my chest. My tattoos.

Philip spent three years in the mid-1960s in Cappagh Orthopedic Hospital, undergoing several operations. In 1983 further complications from his childhood radium treatment resulted in his leg being amputated below the knee. Problems persisted, requiring a further amputation in 1993. Bradley's experience lends context to Casey's. Philip lived with disability for his lifetime and made a point of working for the rights of people with disabilities. Also, as I learned from listening to him, he was also very interested in the lives of people who suffered from mental health issues as well, and understanding the experiences of those who had been abused in institutions, such as his long-time friend Paddy Doyle (author of *The God Squad*).

Sonya Freeman Loftis has noted that 'disability studies grew in tandem with the disability rights movement, and disability studies approaches to literature have increased in popularity since the 1990s.' Disability has begun to be taken seriously by literary and cultural scholars. Writers who live with disabilities have been able to speak of their experience. Barbara Rosenblum has written that 'when you have cancer, you have a new body every day, a body that may or may not have a relationship to the body you had the day before,' a comment that clearly illustrates the degree of difficulty that the disabled face in their lives. In context, it could be argued that Philip Casey's body was different each day. Imagine how difficult this made each day for him. At the heart of the life of someone with cancer is uncertainty, as Rebecca Housel explains:

Lots of questions. No answers. I've made a discovery though, now being an expert on questions without answers. The question of why is always irrelevant. The only question is *why not*. Why not? Why not die? Why not get sick? Why not get well? Why not travel to Australia? Why not live every moment to the fullest? Why not. Not why.

Reading first-hand accounts provided by writers in *Bodies of Truth: Personal Narratives on Illness, Disability and Medicine* and *Staring Back: The Disability Experience from the Inside Out* provides fresh insight into the ways that the disabled are forced to live in this world. We learn about how disability is defined by people who are not themselves disabled, who in effect are colonisers. Freeman Loftis notes that 'the power to define disability is generally controlled by able-bodied medical authorities.' She adds that 'it is all too common for adults with disabilities to be treated as though they were children.'

I can't pretend to understand Philip's own deepest thoughts on his disabilities and the issues he encountered living with them, but I did observe how he dealt with them in the public sphere. In one of the studies of disability, the writer Mark O'Brien asked Stephen Hawking if he felt 'frustration, rage at being disabled', to which Hawking replied, 'I have been lucky. I don't have anything to be angry about.' Philip Casey shared Hawking's attitude, I think. Both Hawking and Casey were able to be mobile in the world, to cross physical and metaphorical borders, and this sense of being able to be on the move rather than fixed in one place makes a difference to how a person with a disability might feel regarding his/her disability, as Hawking points out. Furthermore, both men are defined by their work rather than by their disability, though the two can never be fully separated.

Years after my Irish Writers Centre faux pas, I found this observation that Sonya Freeman Loftis provides in *Shakespeare and Disability* Studies, 'when people with disabilities say that access to theaters can be an emotional, validating, and humanizing experience, they are not engaging in hyperbole.' Yes, I understand it better now.

On the one hand, I see more clearly why disabled people can be so angry when access is denied them. It is an issue of civil rights and fairness and everyone being provided with an equal chance, or the failure thereof. On the other hand, when proper access is provided for disabled people, they feel both empowered and engaged. Given the level of my ignorance that evening in Dublin, Philip's reprimand was quite mild. Of course, it was Philip's style to be gentle in the way that the best teachers are.

Loftis, and many other authors who have a disability, like to disclose their disability to readers 'as a common critical maneuve' though this is something that Philip Casey did not do. He was a writer, and that was enough. He sought material and inspiration from many places, the well he drew from had disparate sources. To be called a writer is the ideal label for most, adding adjectives can be confining for an author's imagination and can limit his/her appeal as Eavan Boland explained so eloquently *in Object Lessons*. But other creative writers have taken a different tack as Alice Wong observes in *Disability Visibility: First Person Stories from the 21st Century*. 'In 2016, novelist Nicola Griffith tweeted a comment with other disabled writers with the hashtag #CripLit.' Philip was on Twitter: I wonder if he saw this and what he thought of it.

Disability does play a role in his work, notably in *The Fabulists* through the character of Mungo, who has damaged his arm in a fire. Also, in the volume of poetry *The Year of the Knife*, where Philip pays homage to Frida Kahlo, an artist with whom he shared so much – in dealing with adversity and in artistic outlook. Joan Tollifson, who was born without her right hand and half of her right arm, has written that 'being disabled is a deep wound, a source of pain.' Since first reading her essay, I have carried this sentence around with me. It is both simple, in how it is stated, understated I suppose, but it is also weighty and sad and terrifying. It is such a nakedly honest and moving statement. Then, Tollifson takes a different track by arguing that 'like all wounds, it is also a gift. As Eastern wisdom has always known, it is hard to tell good luck from bad luck ... Life is the way it is, not the way we wish it was, and disability is a constant embodiment of this truth.' A disciple of Shunryu Suzuki like many other US West Coast writers, she declares 'I am grateful for this koan of one arm, even though it is not always pleasant or easy. It teaches me to appreciate the miracle of what is, to feel affection for my actual life.'

Again, I will admit that I know little about what Philip Casey thought of his disability. For sure, he got around town, travelled widely, lived overseas, seemed to know everybody and to be aware of those he hadn't met. I do believe that, like Tollifson, he felt a deep affection for his own life, for the lives of his friends, like me, and for the planet, for Philip was an early eco warrior.

He was also a pioneer in digital media. He founded, created, and curated the Irish Writers Online website, the first such resource in Ireland. He wrote entries for all Irish writers, including writers from the diaspora, and it was very popular with readers and scholars. In fact, it was an ideal and trustworthy place to begin research. The writer Patrick Chapman is certain that Philip Casey was way ahead of his time in developing digital media projects because he understood how useful new technologies could be to authors. Working together Chapman and Casey set-up irishliteraryrevival.com as a vehicle to make writers' out of print books available in a digital format. Each book was made available with the author's permission. As Chapman notes, 'I registered the URL and Philip built the site on WordPress'. The books were distributed for free under a Creative Commons license. When writers' works became more easily available through other platforms, Casey moved on to found eMaker Editions which he worked on alongside his continuing curation of Irish

Writers Online. The latter was quite an undertaking with new writers being added all the time and existing entries needing updating. As Chapman observes, Philip was a pioneer in the field, 'He found it liberating, as a man living with disability, to be able to take charge of things from home. He found the internet a game changer – liberating for everyone, not just him.'

Writing *Shakespeare and Disability Studies*, Sonya Freeman Loftis notes that 'It is difficult for me to navigate to and from and around the campus library – almost everything I read as I was researching this book came to me electronically (via interlibrary loan or kindle ebook.' The writing and research project that Philip was working on for more than a decade before he passed away was concerned with the history of slavery, particularly the Irish involvement in it. Like Freeman Loftis, Casey was able to do the research from home thanks to computers and broadband. This work is yet to be published.

Suzanne Bost's research in the Gloria Anzaldúa archives and on her published work presents us with opportunities to align Casey's and Anzaldúa's work. She points out that Anzaldúa was disabled by 'severe hormonal imbalance and Type 1 diabetes.' Anzaldúa's 'diabetes brought about sudden changes in blood sugar, dizziness, extreme fatigue, bleeding eyes, and the threat of amputation.' Anzaldúa 'felt as though I had been transformed into an alien other and it was cannibalizing my flesh from the inside.' As a theorist of decolonisation, specifically as it related to ideas of race, nation and gender, Anzaldúa was disinclined to accept how disability was defined by governments, institutions and medical professionals. To accept such definitions meant being imprisoned or colonised both by them and by their creators. As Bost points out, Anzaldúa pushed in another direction, 'refusing to fix bodies with labels (including the label "disabled"). Anzaldúa accepted mystical encounters, unknown worlds, and interspecies minglings without judgement.'

Perhaps Philip Casey's position was more nuanced than Anzaldúa's. On the one hand, he pushed hard for the rights of disabled people as a matter of fairness and practicality; however, on the other hand, he resisted as fiercely as Anzaldúa did being colonised by the term. Anzaldúa's mysticism, as Bost points out, was rooted in Aztec legend and committed 'to Coatlicue, the Aztec goddess of creation and destruction, and her disloyal daughter, the moon goddess Coyolxauhqui,' and underlined by ideas of dismemberment and regeneration. To Anzaldúa's point of view, the body itself was in a *nepantla* or liminal state and might evolve. She was interested in the non-human and reconnecting people with it. Humanism, she felt, had broken the link between the human and non-human.

Correspondingly, there is evidence in Philip Casey's poetry of a reaching beyond the terrestrial towards the heavens, an interest in cosmology that perhaps helped facilitate his later engagements with the digital world and the internet. Anzaldúa searched in myths while Casey sought the stars: "the planets and stars become friends/until I'm blown to pieces, to pieces/in a celestial accident" (from 'The Planets and Stars Become Friends', *Those Distant Summers*, 1980). Though Anzaldúa can be quite prescriptive regarding how her work should be applied by others, she does accept that 'the border is a historical and metaphorical site.' Clearly, people with disabilities must negotiate borders in complex ways.

For the able-bodied person, a staircase in the public building can be the safe path that leads upstairs to a book launch or party. For a person with a physical disability, the reality may be quite different. If there is some enlightenment, this border is erased by a sign pointing towards an elevator. If not, a man or woman is denied access, told to go home. Philip attended many literary events in the Irish Writers Centre, navigating the stairs with his crutches and his everlasting good humour: there is still no elevator in the building.

Philip and Katie Donovan at the Irish Writers Centre

Joseph Woods

IN THE VILLA PALAGONIA
for Philip Casey 1950–2018

Sicily, and poetry that brought us together, Philip.
A first outing for me on the poetry lark,
while you and a few of the others were veterans
but all of us, unjaded and alert to the island's mystery.

I can still hear our shuffle, mutterings and laughter
in the empty ballroom of the grotesque Villa Palagonia,
and imagined dancers caught in the cut-glass ceilings above.
And then, much later in the Winding Stair,

all those readings you rallied to, above and beyond
the call, your handsome head, a face in the crowd, still there.
Last year, I found a pair of crutches in our attic, discarded
by the previous tenants and I can hear you drolly respond,

'And what calibre of detonation did they bring, Joe?'
Your lifted eyebrow and deep uncynical laughter.

Enda Wyley

FIRST READING, FIRST MEETING
on first meeting Philip Casey, March 1990

It's March 1990 and I am clambering up the old wooden stairs of The Winding Stair Bookshop on Dublin's Ormond Quay. I'm 24 years old and, though writing since a teenager, have never read my poems at a poetry reading before.

Tonight, things are going to change. I've been invited by the poet and publisher Dermot Bolger to read some of my new poems at the launch of an anthology he's just brought out of up-and-coming young poets called *12 Bar Blues.*

It's the start of a new decade, a time when anyone interested in writing poetry knows about Dermot Bolger. He runs the coolest publishing house in Dublin. He's from Finglas and set up Raven Arts Press when he was only 18 and he publishes new voices, poets I've been reading voraciously – Sara Berkeley, Nuala Ní Dhomhnaill. Paul Durcan, also published by Raven, says this new wave of poets has nothing in common, 'except dissidence and originality.' Amongst them is a poet, whose book, *After Thunder*, I've only just begun to read, Philip Casey. Fresh, humane poems that draw me to them. I wonder will I meet him tonight?

The top of the stairs opens out to a wide, high-ceilinged room which is noisy with activity. The bearded, jumper-clad Dermot Bolger welcomes me, thrusts a copy of the new anthology into my hand. I see my name emblazoned on the cover with twelve other poets – Conor O'Callaghan, Heather Brett, Patrick Chapman ... – and it makes me feel nervous and proud all at once. I'm a shy young poet but quietly determined in my urge to write. Suddenly this evening feels intimidating but somehow important to me.

A tall, thin young man is buzzing about, chatting to everyone and helping Dermot set up the room for the reading. He introduces himself. He's a poet called Pat Boran and he has poems in the book too. Would I mind helping? Of course not. I'm feeling awkward and doing something seems like a great idea. If anything, it might stop me feeling nervous. I begin to put out chairs for this buzzing gathering of poets, their friends and family.

My sister arrives with a bunch of roses. Well done, she says, and I feel happy but embarrassed by her gesture, don't quite know what to do with the flowers. Then a voice behind me. There's a seat here if you want to sit down?

He's a handsome man – he looks about forty – with a smiling face, dark sideburns and a thick head of hair. He has settled himself in the front row, with one leg extended outwards and a crutch balanced under a relaxed arm. *I'm Philip*, he says. *Philip Casey. Are you reading tonight?*

The room is filling fast, and I've lost my sister in the crowd, so I take him up on his offer and sit down beside him. When he asks my name, he's enthusiastic, says he's read and liked my poems and I tell him I've just been reading his poems too and really like his work. We begin to chat some more. He has a quiet, richly textured voice and it relaxes me, makes me feel a bit braver. Maybe I will have the courage to read my poems, after all.

I look at his leg, say I'm very sorry he's injured. But will he get better soon? He tosses his head back and smiles. We both laugh together, though I'm not quite sure why. Have I said something funny? Maybe later he will explain.

Dermot comes around with a list. It's the order of the reading and because my surname begins with 'w' I'm to read last, he explains. My face pales and Philip notices, leans in. *Is this your first reading, then?* When I nod, he immediately says, *don't be afraid. You'll be great.*

The room settles and a hush descends. Poems rise like bright new birds in the room. Somehow, I manage to listen to every single poem that long night, and when my name is called, I feel Philip at my side nudge me up.

More than anything it is his gentle kindness that pushes me forward and I feel myself grow in confidence, my poems reaching out to everyone in the room but especially to this poet who I've only just met, who sits in the front row, his words of encouragement willing me on.

At last, it's over, clapping and I sit down. *See?* Philip says, as the crowd disperses, my first reading done and dusted. *I told you it would be all right.*

Grace Wynne-Jones

LISTENING TO PHILIP'S VOICE

I sometimes told Philip that he could make big bucks from doing advertising voiceovers – a joke, of course, that sort of stuff wouldn't even remotely tempt him. But he did have the most marvellous voice. It was just the right timbre, was warm and genuine like himself. Just listening to his voice soothed me. Thankfully, he put it to good use when he gave public readings from his brilliant, and acclaimed, novels and poetry. He was "much loved", and "at the heart of the Irish literary world" said the *Irish Times*. So true.

But, since he was a cherished friend, there are so many other things to mention. Something from the patchwork that comes to mind is his laughter, it was wholehearted, abundant and infectious.

So, one of life's great pleasures became making him laugh. He had a highly tuned sense of the ridiculous, which was a delight in conversation. And, of course, he often made people laugh heartily himself. Sometimes, when Philip was comforting me about some difficult situation, he'd joke: *Feck 'em all bar Maisie, she makes the curranty cakes*. It is now part of my treasure trove of quotations.

Philip was an absolute whizz at software and computers. While very deftly roaming the vast expanses of the internet, he unearthed a huge store of important, and often neglected, information.

Master wordsmith that he was, with books to write or research, he was very generous with his time and a great champion of fellow writers. He even founded, and maintained, Irish Writers Online, a great Irish literary resource. And he urged me to get a website, offered to design it for me. This he very kindly did. Philip lived up to the quote he often included at the end of his emails 'Be kind, for everyone you meet is fighting a hard battle' (Ian McLaren).

He was also modest and unassuming. Looking through some past tweets – Philip still has a twitter account – very few are about himself. Instead, concerns about social injustice in all its forms are evident. His other sharings reflect his broad vision, and large range of interests.

Today, I reposted Philip's pinned tweet – I have done this a number of times in the past. In it he thanks Terry McDonagh for a tweet that says: *I have read all three of Philip's novels and each one, in its own way, remains unforgettable ... I return to them again and again.*

In his award-winning writing, and in his brave life, Philip did not shy away from difficult topics – he wanted to explore and shed light on them. Of course, he was no stranger to difficulty himself. He met his considerable physical challenges with remarkable courage. His personal suffering prompted even deeper empathy and insight.

Diving deep into the story of Irish slavery and servitude, as he did in his later years, was fuelled by his humanitarianism, his sense of injustice for subject people. True to form, he did much revelatory historical research. When we talked, he often mentioned some intriguing detail he'd uncovered. It was a huge and important task. It would be wonderful if this treasure trove of historical information found its way into print.

I have never known someone to have so many friends, both in Ireland and abroad. His book launches were bulging with kinship. Visitors from near and far came to his welcoming, unfussy home on Arran Street East. They were met with the same soft swing of the red door, the same warm, comradely smile.

I was one of his visitors, from Bray, not Germany or America. To me, Philip and his comforting home were a joy. The hurly burly of O'Connell Street was just down the road, but time had a different texture in Philip's charming sitting-room. Arrayed on shelves were many books on a huge range of topics and his trusty laptop was on a table by the front window. Also on the table was an exotic plant with thick green foliage, it stayed there year after year.

Seated on his comfy sofa, I could stare into space if I felt like it. Philip was steady, easygoing company. He accepted you just as you were; there was no social pressure to be clever or interesting. A trip to the kitchen might reveal culinary delights. He was a regular at Temple Bar Food Market, and had a refined palate. He might chuckle at being lauded for his refined palate. But sure, why not add it to the patchwork, it's true.

And, of course, there were convivial chats over tea – loose leafed and steaming in mugs. I don't think we often conversed about bookish matters, though I had huge admiration for his literary talent. Sometimes one just wants to shoot the breeze, ask inconsequential things, such as whether he'd got around to wearing that very swish designer jacket. I still don't know the answer. A charity shop discovery, it was fun to jovially speculate on the events that might require it. And, of course, his much-loved family sometimes popped into the conversation: his brothers Peter and John, and his sister, Karina. Dear Karina, like Philip, has kindly encouraged my own writing.

Back in 2005, I included some lines from a poem by Philip in an article for the *Irish Times*. The article was about the velocity of the Celtic Tiger. Philip's poem, 'The Time of No Time', was taken from his poetry collection *Dialogue in Fading Light*. In the poem's last lines he writes:

> daily we spent hours
> in the isolation units of our cars,
> stuck in the loop of the round trip.
> It was the time of no time.

As usual, he found just the right words.

Philip was a cherished presence in many lives. A much loved, and much missed man. I have never met anyone else like him.

Philip Casey

SELECTED (AND NEW) WRITING

Philip in his office
photo by Matt Kavanagh, Irish Times

AUTOBIOGRAPHY

for John and Peter

I was eight when I dreamt
of a dazzling whitewashed wall
and a river flanked by trees.
Three years later they were part
of our new lives, and we saw
the river wash green weed, and smoke
from the cottage against the hill
betray the direction of the breeze.

The genial owner of the farm
by the river taught us to kill
trout, before he and our father
bargained, and we, in high spirits
when the deal was done, ran back
to the sparkling water to try our skill.

When all three of us had tired
we lay against a grassy brow,
taking in the feverish blue
of the mountain in mid-summer.

In another month, we would float
through the heat of wheat fields,
being razed by a hired machine,
and roam the stubbled earth.

Settled into our first winter there,
we watched the rain race across
the fields from Annagh and Croghan.
The earth had become hostile and bare,
and we knew the chill of loss
as hill and mountain turned to stone.

HOSPITAL BED

This bed upon which I lie
has taken so many bodies upon it
that it's fit to hitch up its sheets
and lean its backrest against
a dimly-lit lamp post.
"Do you want a good time,
handsome?
I can fix you a *petit-mort*
before you know where you are!"

DAILY BREAD

for my neighbours

This morning, the sky cleared to reveal Spring.
I went to the bakery hard by the market
and the streets were vital in the clear light.
A woman pushed a pram, her son holding on,
and she was happy to be with her children.
We dodged Japanese forklifts shifting oranges
from Jaffa, apples from Spain, potatoes from Rush.
Adjusting her shades, a driver reclined,
enjoying the breeze in the hold of her van.
The district was thronged, and juggernauts
edged their way through a street made for horses.
Amid merciless banter, a man was absorbed
in his racing page, reckoning his luck
as a dray-horse relished abandoned cabbage.

Arran Street East, 1990

DIALOGUE IN FADING LIGHT

In the dead of night I watch the moon.
Emptied of everything but your grace,
night long I stare at its mask of light.

I recall ice dripping into a drain.
The drain was deep and the sound faint,
the unpredictable drip a portent.

Our sun is many times the size of the earth,
and red giants like Betelgeuse dwarf the sun,
and for all I know, Betelgeuse is a mote
in the scale of Creation. Yet we belong.

The eye craves rhythm and colour.
There's no healing or ease
in a vista where nothing coheres.

You renewed me by losing yourself
to our deepening dialogue in fading light.
To star dust we shall return.

A pink moon rose as we parted,
its presence over the rooftops a focus,
a celestial light through the dust of pollution,
composing all that had been in isolation.

from

THE FABULISTS (1994)

Mungo got himself a magazine from the table and flicked through it. It was a month since he had his last certificate, and his arm had improved dramatically since then because of Tess. He closed the magazine. What had Tess to do with it and where had that thought sprung from? He had worked very hard at building up the strength in his arm and he had done that because ... of Tess. He put the ridiculous notion out of his mind and tried to imagine his interview, although maybe that wasn't the right word. There would only be one view. He tried to work out the sums of entitlement he had talked about with Connie, and if his family would be worse off, but he couldn't grapple with this. Very often the professionals didn't know for sure.

His turn came and he sat before a man of late middle-age who seemed upset about something. Perhaps he had sciatica, or gout. Perhaps he hated his job. Mungo wanted this over with as soon as possible.

'I was at my doctor a month ago –'

'Yes, I know.' The doctor looked up from Mungo's records, but Mungo was determined, although he didn't want his anger to show.

'I've been working really hard on it since, and it's responded very well.' Mungo knew that 'responded' was a good medical term since Aidan's time in hospital. 'Especially in the last week or so. You could say I'm fit in other words.'

The doctor, who had been reading throughout Mungo's speech, looked up again, and stared at him.

'I could, but then again I might not. Take off your shirt.'

Mungo burned, but did as he was told, glancing at the nurse who had busied herself at a separate desk. After a brief examination, Mungo dressed, and the doctor ignored him as he wrote his report.

'Well? Am I fit for work?'

'You'll hear in a week or two.'

Mungo shook his head in disbelief, but said nothing, unsure if he was expected to leave or not. He stood. The nurse rose and asked him how he had travelled into town. By bus, he said, and he received a voucher which he could cash in the front office for his return bus fare, and with it, a mildly satisfying theft from the tormenting State, as he had walked in, and he would walk home.

Outside, he took a deep breath, and caressed his ill-got gains in an otherwise empty pocket. He had, perhaps, enough for two cups of tea and a shared bun, and, thinking this, he gave up denying that Tess had been at the back of his mind, that there was a possibility of meeting her in The Winding Stair, and that that was why he found himself walking there.

He spent a pleasant hour in the book café, watching the crowds cross the Ha'penny Bridge, listening to the music and sipping tea long after it had gone cold. He had not bought a slice of fruit cake, in case she came after all. Then depression set in as he realised the futility of his vigil and he left, knowing that all he had to do was walk down the quay and knock on her door. But instead he walked home down Great and Little Strand Streets, Arran Street, Chancery Street, past the old, crumbling distillery into Smithfield. All the way, he was rehearsing the story he would spin for Tess when they next met. Halfway up Smithfield he noticed debris where the travellers' caravans had been. At first he thought that they had dumped rubbish before moving on, but there was something about it that was odd. He went across to see for himself. All that was left of the caravan was a rectangular heap of ashes, an axle, and an aluminium chimney.

from

THE WATER STAR (1999)

When Brendan had been alone in England and Hugh had lived with his mother on the mountainside, he had missed his father so much that Máire, his mother, had often come across him trailing a saucepan along the bed of the stream, searching for gold. The thought of his mother cut through him. Why it had upset her, he had never discovered, but he persisted. Everyone said there had been gold on the mountain in the days of the landlord. He wasn't sure what gold looked like, but knew that if he could find one small nugget, or even grains, his father could return and stay.

Recently he had missed her a great deal. The pain of it struck him from nowhere, when he was working, or crossing the street, or buying groceries. Why had the hurt come now, he wondered, so long after she had died?

The hard week caught up with him, and the upper-class English voices drifted far away.

The next morning he woke at nine, confused. Brendan was snoring and would doubtless do so until the afternoon. That's how he managed to work like a horse all week, the old shagger. Hugh felt as if he hadn't slept all night, although it was a long time since he had slept so well, but he struggled out of bed and washed. He lay wearily back on the bed again for some time, but then he dressed in his Sunday suit, and struggled with his tie before he got it tolerably right. He could never remember the knack and only got it out through luck.

The fine morning seemed to clear his head, and as he crossed Holloway Road at the zebra above the hospital, and turned into Tollington Way, he found himself whistling loudly. He waited until he had walked out of earshot of anyone who may have heard him, and began again, this time softly. He reached the T-junction at

Hornsey Road, turned left and then right into Tollington Park, past Sarah's house. He looked to see if Deirdre, Sarah's daughter, was waiting for him at the window as she sometimes was. Sarah didn't go to Mass, so he assumed she was a Protestant, though Deirdre went to the Catholic school across the way.

He assumed this even though Brendan didn't bother any more either.

When he was a child, he had always thought that London had no hills. He remembered this as he walked up the incline of Tollington Park, past the large Protestant church and into Everleigh Street, where the Irish faithful were congregating. Hugh was perversely proud that his church had a corrugated iron roof, in contrast to its grand Protestant neighbour. No matter that Catholic churches in Ireland were of good stone and slate, the poverty of this one made him feel a cut above the Prods, morally speaking. As he dipped his fingers in the holy water font, he spied Mrs Dempsey with her husband and children.

After Mass, as they queued to get an Irish paper, they spotted him as he used his sweet ration at the hucksters, and waved, but small talk terrified him, so he smiled and moved on quickly. It meant he was too early for Sarah's class, so he walked for a while into Upper Tollington Park, before doubling back. Along with the heat, his self-consciousness had made him sweat, and he thought with relish of the two bitters he had had the night before.

He arrived early at Sarah's, which he knew she didn't encourage, but he needed a drink of water. Deirdre greeted him as always.

'It's hot, Deirdre,' he said.

'Would you like a drink of water?'

'I'd kill for it.'

'Oh, there's no need to do that,' she said primly.

'Here's your sweets,' he whispered, following her inside.

'Thanks!' she said, her face lighting up, and she rushed in to hand them to Sarah, who was in the kitchen washing vegetables. Without a word, she took the sweets from Deirdre and put them away until after lunch.

'You're early,' she said.

'I'm sorry, Sarah. I had a terrible thirst.'

Deirdre squeezed in beside her mother to get the cup of water.

'Well, don't make a habit of it,' she said. 'The others'll think you're my favourite.'

from

THE FISHER CHILD (2001)

Montserrat, late 1798–1802

All went easily for some days. While travelling to
Hamburg in calm summer waters, he had learned to furl
and unfurl sail, and now, being quick at whatever he was
sent to do, the mate, though he showed no favour, was
only harsh to him in speech, and Hugh thought of making
the sea his life, away from cursed, disputed land. At night
he amused himself by watching the moon dance about the
sky as the ship rolled over the waves. Then, off the north-
west coast of Spain, they were assailed by a thunderstorm,
the lightning making day of night, the lit sea swelling
around them like a succession of moving hills, and once
again he knew the sour taste of fear. As he stood by his
watch, he thought that he would accept his fate, but if they
survived, he would never set foot on a ship again. The
decision calmed him.

By dawn, the sea was quiet. The men had talked of
hurricanes in the Caribbean, where they were bound, but
the season had passed. There would be no more storms on
this voyage, though he would almost wish for one as they
crossed the doldrums with barely a lungful of air to draw
breath.

*

They dropped anchor off Montserrat at dawn. As Hugh
came on deck, he stopped to look at the beauty of the
island, set like a green stone in the turquoise sea, its
mountains pinning it to the ocean floor. During the voyage
Will Thomson had told him he had been here before, that
it was an English colony won back from the French of late,

but that it was an Irish island. The mate woke Hugh from his wonder with a roar, and he set to work.

As the boats approached them from a stony beach, carrying small mountains of barrels, he saw that a few among the crews were white, but mostly they were black.

'I only ever seen one black man before,' Hugh said.

'Where you been all your life, lad? Them's not men. Them's slaves. And not just any slaves,' Will said, as if to challenge Hugh. 'Them's the slaves of the Irish.'

'The slaves of the Irish ...' Lord Edward Fitzgerald, the United Irish leader who had been killed resisting arrest, had kept a black slave in his mansion. Hugh had heard that in Hamburg, but had thought nothing of it. Now he was confused.

They exchanged cargo, and the islanders rowed back. They were a good distance out from the shore, but Hugh could see one group wade out to take the barrels from the boat and carry them to the white checker on the stony beach, as another group waded out with barrels of sugar cane and coffee, and other goods he had never heard of. They worked that way, back and forth.

'Are there any black women?' Hugh asked Will.

'Oho, boy, you can bet your sweet life. I had me a black woman once,' he said, leering, but Hugh didn't rise to that. He was having second thoughts about settling here. He didn't like the idea of slaves. He liked even less the prospect of working among black men every day, keeping the face of Anthony King forever before him.

When the merchandise was exchanged and secure, the captain was rowed ashore.

from

THE COUPLA (2015)

THE LONG SHADOWS

After they had come down from the buzz of swimming with dolphins, breathing under water and meeting a whale, the Coupla could barely stand up on the pier. Their father finished mooring and securing Pudda, and marched home ahead of them in silence.

'We were riding fish,' Kate said to Danny.

'They're not fish.'

'What are they, then?'

'They have lungs like us, so they're mammals,' said Danny. 'But I know what you mean. Are we weird?'

'You know we are. Off the scale,' Kate replied. 'No wonder we've no friends. No real friends, I mean.'

'You're my best friend, Kate,' Danny said.

Her head swung around in surprise.

'I'm calling mine Zip,' he said quickly.

'Calling what Zip?' And then she knew what he was talking about. 'Hey, I wanted to call mine Zip.'

'You could always call him Lip,' Danny said with a superior grin.

'Very smart. He'll always be Nip to me.'

'And the other fella?' Danny asked.

'Oh, he has to be Smiler.'

'Smiler he is.'

That night they could only sleep in fits and starts. It was all very well naming the dolphins, but that was avoiding some very big questions.

When Danny woke at three in the morning, he needed a drink of water, but when he got halfway down the stairs, wondering why the lights were still on, he saw his father sitting by the fire, drinking a glass of whiskey. He doubled back and carefully opened Kate's door.

'Kate, are you awake?'

'Yes.'

'You know how that first day we went to Imaire,' Danny said, 'and we thought everything had changed. Well, everything's really changed now.'

'I know,' said Kate.

'Do you feel a lot – I mean a lot – older?'

'A lot,' said Kate. 'I always wanted to be older, but now it's scary.'

'And we laughed.'

She didn't answer. There was no need. Danny closed her door and stood on the landing for a while, one foot against the wall, still trying to take in what had happened. It was all bloody scary. In fact, scary wasn't the word for it.

At breakfast, their father was thoughtful.

'Coupla,' he said, 'don't tell anyone what happened yesterday.'

'No, Dad,' Kate said. As if they would.

'They wouldn't understand,' their father said.

'It's our secret,' Danny said.

'Good.'

'Can we go and see the dolphins on Sunday?' Kate asked.

'No.'

'But Dad!'

'No buts. You were right – it's dangerous at this time of year. I don't know what got into me. We almost all drowned, remember?'

'But Dad, the dolphins will –'

'I said, no buts!' He stopped at the door for a moment. 'Maybe in the Spring.' Then he went out.

'The Spring,' Danny moaned.

'That's a million years away,' Kate said, making a face.

'I'm not waiting that long,' Danny said. 'I can't.'

from
HISTORIES OF THE IRISH
(unpublished to date)

The Plains of Ireland

At the urging of my good friend, the classicist and novelist Ronan Sheehan, I travelled with him and several other guests to an event in Teltown in County Meath in October 2011. My role was to read, in its English translation, a medieval Gaelic poem telling the fate of Tailtiu, Queen of the Firbolg.

West of Teltown, about forty-five minutes by car, is Brú na Bóinne, which at almost eight square kilometres is the largest megalithic site in the world. *Bóinne* is Irish for the Boyne river and is named for the ancient river goddess Boann. The word *Brú* has been interpreted as Palace, but it also has the meaning of womb, belly, bowels, so Brú na Bóinne could be interpreted as the 'belly or womb of Boann'. Bordered on one side by a bend in the Boyne river, it dates from 3,800 to 2,200 BCE.

Its most famous monument is Newgrange, constructed some 5,200 years ago. Weather permitting, the sun floods its passage tomb at the winter solstice. Knowth and Dowth, of similar size, and which complete a triangle with Newgrange, are slightly younger but also have precise astronomical functions. Knowth itself has some 120 engraved kerbstones, and alone accounts for a quarter of Europe's megalithic art, including the oldest known map of the moon, discovered by Dr Philip Stooke as late as 1999, and thought to be 5,000 years old. Placing his markings over a picture of the full moon, Dr Stooke was amazed to find that they lined up, from the *Mare Humorum* across to the *Mare Crisium*.

So these were sophisticated people, most likely members of a European elite which included astronomers and engineers. In Irish legend they are associated with the Tuatha de Danann, or the People of the goddess Danu. Aengus, the Tuatha de Danann god of youth, love and poetry, was said to reside at Newgrange. His father was the Dagda, also known as Ollathair, or All-Father, and his mother was Boann.

Returning to Teltown and its environs, the ramparts of Queen Tailtiu date to at least six hundred years before our era, though the old texts, which it must be said were prone to exaggeration and indeed were used for propaganda purposes, insist that the first Battle of Moytura between the Tuatha de Danann and the Firbolgs took place in 1272 BC. According to the translation of the poem I read at Teltown, Tailtiu, Queen of the Firbolg, was enslaved after the defeat of her husband, but on her deathbed she demanded of the men of Erin, 'to whom she was in bondage,' that they host Funeral Games in her memory.

And so it came to pass. The Tailteann Games, with their accompanying great and peaceful Fair and match-making ceremonies, were held for at least two millennia, and we were in Teltown to celebrate their presumed similarity in age and purpose to the Olympic Games of Greece. Before a packed audience – which included several native Irish speakers – in a large room at Teltown House, where like poets of old we enjoyed lavish hospitality, Pindar, the laureate of the Olympic Games, was read in Greek and English by Dr Vasilis Politis of TCD. His colleague, Dr Brendan O'Byrne, gave us a talk on the original Olympics. In the second half of the evening, Ronan Sheehan read the first three verses of Tailtiu's story in the original medieval Irish.

Then it was my turn to read all fifteen pages of the 19th century English translation. Parts of it are obscure with complex Christian overlays, and I expected some coughing and shuffling of feet. All I could hear, however, was the sound of my voice and the wind-lashed rain against the window behind me. *Dindshenchas* is the Irish for lore of place, and I was reading the archaic lore in verse of Teltown.

The Metrical *Dindshenchas* was part of a great 19th century, fifty year effort by German and Irish scholars to translate the surviving manuscripts of medieval Gaelic Ireland. Much had already been lost, although a treasure trove of stories had come down to us in the surviving oral tradition – despite the devastation of the Famine. Sponsored by the British Government, which in its incarnation of previous centuries had suppressed this very culture, the translations opened up a grand literary, legal and historical vista previously hidden in a language which even contemporary Irish speakers could no longer fully understand.

The Irish Slave-owners in Montserrat

The Irish-dominated island of Montserrat produced the largest single compensation package in the Leewards after Emancipation. Donald H. Akenson estimated that in 1824, one-third of the slaves on Montserrat were owned by five Catholic families with strong Irish connections. The largest slave-owner on the island was Queely Shiell, an Irish Catholic whose family had purchased land on Montserrat sometime after 1729. Akenson estimates that in 1824 he had 656 African slaves; ten years later he claimed for 913 slaves, receiving £14,855. Akenson lists the seventh largest slaveowners on Montserrat as being Clement and Mathew Kirwan, with a total of 284 slaves. Ten years later Clement was dead, but his widow and executrix, Elizabeth Kirwan, was awarded £1,655 for 115 slaves on the Waterworks Estate, and £3333 for 200 enslaved on the Farm estate, along with Mathew Kirwan, who was also awarded £2,081 for 123 enslaved. The greater Kirwan family also had property on Antigua. Nicholas Kirwan, a City of Dublin merchant and executor of Patrick Kirwan received £2854 on the Bendals estate in Antigua for 225 enslaved. Like a number of the Irish who enriched themselves in the Caribbean, their wealth was invested in houses in England, not Ireland. Clement Kirwan's will, for example, lists his address as Kendal Lodge, Essex. As emancipation became inevitable, planters left land to their sons and slaves to their daughters. In Jamaica, amongst the smallholding women with Irish names who claimed compensation were Brigit Garvey (8 slaves, though her father or brother had 74), Elizabeth Anne Carroll (7 slaves), Elizabeth Geoghegan (6 slaves – the Geoghegan family appear to have had slaves on several estates), Eleanor Tierney (10 slaves), Mary O'Sullivan (5 slaves), Murphy (four slaves) and Mary Anne Connolly. Not all of the Irish claimants were resident in the Caribbean. Slave owners across a wide social spectrum and resident in Ireland received compensation. Peter Daly, of Dalysgrove, Galway, received £2,318 for 113 slaves on Daly's Grove estate in Manchester, Jamaica. Not all of the claimants were successful. Michael Lindsey of Hollymount, County Mayo, unsuccessfully claimed £6,212 for 206 slaves on his Telescope Estate in Grenada. In all, one hundred and eighteen names are listed as resident in Ireland.

Montserrat was – and still is – known as 'The Emerald Isle' of the Caribbean and celebrates St Patrick's Day. However, the celebration is ambivalent. 18th century Montserratian slaves chose St Patrick's Day, 1768, to rebel against their Irish masters, who, acting on a tip from a household slave, thwarted the rebellion and executed eighteen of the leaders. As the overworked land began to fail in the early 19th century, many of the descendants of Irish slave owners sold up their plantations and moved to Virginia or England. From Cromwellian times, Irish indentured servants had moved from Barbados (where they were badly treated), to Jamaica, where they became smallholders and mostly small-time slave owners, although there were some Protestant Irish who had bigger properties. Slave holder names in Jamaica included O'Dwyer, O'Hara, O'Conner, Talbot, Coulthurst, Herbert, Gregory, Martin, Madden, Forde, Richards, Dobbs, and de la Touche. Tulio O'Neill O'Keffe, and Arturo O'Neill O'Keffe (i.e. O'Keefe), who were born in Saint Croix in the 1780s of Irish parents and descended from the O'Neill's of the Fews, moved to Puerto Rico with their slaves and plantation equipment with another Irish planter residing in Saint Croix, Tomás Armstrong. The O'Neills of Puerto Rico had large slave plantations. Slavery in Puerto Rico was not abolished until 1873. A similar pattern followed there, with the slaves obliged to work for their former masters for an extra three years. The owners were compensated at 35 million pesetas per slave. When R.R. Madden resigned his post in Jamaica in November 1834, he and his wife, accompanied by their son, sailed to New York and arrived on December 6th. Accompanied by 'a very respectable man of colour' to whom he had a letter of introduction from Jamaica, he attended service in Anthony Street. Apart from himself, the congregation consisted exclusively of about two hundred well-dressed people of colour of both sexes. People of colour, he noted, were excluded from all places of worship, except, he was proud to say, the Roman Catholic churches. As the congregation left, he was assailed by a mob shouting 'No amalgamation,' 'No abolitionists,' and 'Down with all incendiary friends of niggers.' He found that the white population of the northern states where slavery had been abolished hated the freed slaves and their descendants with a ferocity which bordered on the unbelievable. He visited a number of theatres, including the Bowery Theatre, where he saw T.J. Rice, the original 'Jim Crow' and had to endure seven encores of the 'Jim Crow' song and dance. Thomas Dartmouth Rice had been a mediocre actor and light comedian until he heard, according to one account, a negro stage-driver sing the following in Cincinnati in 1830.

Turn about an' wheel about an' do jis so,
An' ebery time I turn about I jump Jim Crow.

His gross stereotype of African Americans made him famous, and he had a number of imitators. He was also the author of a number of successful 'negro farces.' He died in 1860, a decade before the term 'Jim Crow' became synonymous with the racial oppression and segregation laws introduced after the American civil war.

Michael Considine

PHILIP CASEY
BIBLIOGRAPHY

The primary intention of this bibliography is to provide a
comprehensive record of Philip Casey's publications since
his first poem appeared in the late 1960s. Separate sections
have been given over to books, original poems in English,
poems published in journals and poems published in
anthologies. Every attempt has been made to list all of the
books reviewed by Philip during his time as the poetry
reviewer for both *The Sunday Press* and *The Sunday Tribune*
and as an occasional reviewer for other newspapers.
Reviews of Philip's own work are contained in a separate
section. Articles and commentary about Philip's life and
work are listed separately.

In following the generally accepted practice, every
attempt has been made to list the publications in
chronological order within each category. Philip's
involvement with the internet is also noted. Philip would
be amused at the idea that this record of his many
publications should exist in a non-virtual world.

A number of Philip's books have been translated into
other languages, and these too are noted. Because of the
volume and range of Philip's work over fifty years – both
within Ireland and beyond – it is inevitable that there will
oversights and unintended omissions. The responsibility
for this fall solely on the bibliographer.

I have also referred to many articles from local
newspapers circulating in the Wexford area as a means of
showing how Philip's involvement with County Wexford
did not diminish with time but grew stronger. Philip's
energy and creativity extended far beyond the works listed
in this bibliography. Philip was an advocate for a host of
things including the role of the arts and its potential within

the community. He championed the rights of the under-represented in society.

This bibliography is a tangible record of Philip's achievements, but it should be remembered that Philip's natural modesty meant that even his closest friends were not fully aware of the extent and magnitude of his achievements. He produced a remarkable body of work despite constant health difficulties and periods of prolonged hospitalisation.

It is hoped that this bibliography will foster and increase interest in, and appreciation of, Philip Casey's work as poet, novelist, reviewer and historian.

The 'eagle-eyed' reader will notice that some of the bibliographical entries are incomplete. The reason for this is that entries are based on secondary sources as the primary sources were difficult to locate. It was felt the inclusion of these entries was a useful means of drawing the reader's attention to the existence of these publications. In some instances, page numbers are also missing. This is due to a practice mainly in the 1980s of not numbering pages.

Philip with Michael Considine

REMINISCENCES

My Generation, Rock and Roll Remembered: An Imperfect History (Dublin: Lilliput Press, 1996).

Philip contributed his poem 'In Loving Memory of a Country Priest' along with a short recollection of starting school in Monaseed in *Monaseed National School 1913: A book to celebrate 100 hundred years of Monaseed National School* (Monaseed Centenary Committee, 2013).

'From Acid Batteries to an Art Centre' in *Wexford Through its Writers*, edited by Dermot Bolger (Dublin: New Island Books, 1992), pp 15–34.

Cappagh National Orthopaedic Hospital: Celebrating 100 Years (2008).

'Comforts of Youth: Philip Casey on the Sights and Sounds of Childhood', *The Irish Times*, 14 September 2002.

BOOKS
POETRY COLLECTIONS

The Planets and Stars Become Friends (Gorey: Funge Art Centre, 1974), pamphlet.

Those Distant Summers (Dublin: Raven Arts Press, 1980).

After Thunder (Dublin: Raven Arts Press/Buckinghamshire, Colin Smythe, 1985).

The Year of the Knife: Poems 1980–1990 (Dublin: Raven Arts Press, 1991).

Dialogue in Fading Light: New and Selected Poems (Dublin: New Island, 2005).

Tried and Sentenced: Selected Poems, edited by Marion Kelly (Dublin, eMaker Editions, 2014).

NOVELS: THE BANN RIVER TRILOGY

The Fabulists (Dublin: Lilliput Press, 1994). English and American editions published by Serif Fiction in April 1995. Revised edition by eMaker Editions (Dublin: 2014). Also published simultaneously on Kindle and as an ebook.

The Water Star (London: Picador, 1998). Revised edition by eMaker Editions (Dublin, 2014).

The Fisher Child (London: Picador, 2001). Revised edition by eMaker Editions (Dublin, 2014).

The Coupla (Dublin: eMaker Editions, 2015).

TRANSLATIONS OF PHILIP CASEY'S WORK

The Fabulists (Dublin: eMaker Editions, 2015) Japanese edition translated by Noriko Ito.

Die Traumer von Dublin (Munich, Goldman Verlag, 1999).

PLAYS

Sediment Rising (rehearsed reading in the Peacock Theatre, Dublin). Cited in *The Sunday Tribune*, 28 May 1989.

Cardinal (rehearsed reading in the Peacock Theatre, Dublin, and presented at the International Schule in Hamburg). Cited in *The Enniscorthy Guardian*, 18 October 1990.

POEMS PUBLISHED IN JOURNALS

'The Wretched Choirboy' and 'Full Tilt Raindrop'. *Faction* (Funge Arts Centre, nd).

'For Katherine Kavanagh' and 'Thieb' (an experimental prose piece). *The Pleiades Laugh with Paul Funge* (Funge Arts Centre, 1973).

'The Dream Hunter', *The Gorey Detail, No. 2* (Funge Arts Centre, 1978)

'Easter Week' and 'Journey', *The Gorey Detail*, No. 3, edited by Philip Casey (Funge Arts Centre, 1979).

'Serious Sentences about George Molloy', *Funge Arts Centre Broadsheet*, edited by Philip Casey (1979).

'No Words Mean One Thing Only', *Cyphers*, No. 10, Spring, 1979, p. 28.

'Vanishing Awe', Spring *Broadsheet*, Wexford Arts Centre, 1979.

'Victim', 'La Extranjera', 'Those Distant Summers' and 'Fable', *The Cork Review*, March-April, nd, No. 3, pp 10–11.

'Dangerous Love', *The Gorey Detail*, No. 4 (Gorey Arts Centre, 1980).

'In Loving Memory of Maura Laverty', *Cyphers*, No. 12, 1980, pp 8–9.

'Rosa Luxembourg, a Letter from Prison to Sophie Liebknecht', *Gorey Arts Centre Broadsheet*, Easter, 1981.

'Outside Geometry' and 'Yet Again, Farewell', *The Gorey Detail*, No. 5 (Gorey Arts Centre, 1981).

'Into Whiteness', *Cyphers*, No. 17, 1982, p. 35.

'Looking through the Gates at Mount St. Benedict' and 'Marx's Tomb', *The Gorey Detail*, No. 7 (Gorey Arts Centre, 1983).

'Beneath the Veneer', *Cream City Review*, Vol. 9, No. 1 & 2, 1984, p. 66.

'The Walking Shadow', *St Joseph's C.B.S Gorey, 1854–1993* (Gorey, 1993), p. 35.

'The Door' and 'Patterns', *Acorn 3, New Writing*, Dublin Writers Workshop (Autumn, 1993), p. 26.

'The Warm Stone', *Cyphers*, No 48 (2005), pp 59–60.

'Ordinary Mortals', *Poetry Ireland Review*, No 12, p. 62.

'Sunlight of Love', *The Stinging Fly*, Issue 2, Vol. 2 (Autumn/Winter, 2005/06), p. 61.

'The Windfall Oak', *The Scaldy Detail* (Enniscorthy Launchpad, 2005), p. 8.

POEMS PUBLISHED IN NEWSPAPERS

'On Wanting To', *The Irish Press*, 22 November 1980.

'Train to Westport', *The Connacht Tribune*, 7 June 1984.

'Lynwood' and 'New Verse', *Evening Herald*, 9 July 1987.

'The Freedom of June', *The Observer*, 23 March 1990.

'Implications of a Sketch', *The Sunday Tribune*, 27 November 1988.

'The Hotel', *The Irish Times*, 23 May 2009.

POEMS PUBLISHED IN ANTHOLOGIES

'To Dream' and 'This Despicable Village' in *Contemporary Poets of 1971* (London and New York: Regency Press, 1971).

'Autobiography: Dream One', 'Through a Glass Brightly', 'Interstice', 'A Ballet of Life and Death', 'Victim', 'Things Eternal' and 'In Loving Memory of A Country Priest' in *Feathers and Bones: Ten Poets of the Irish Earth,* edited by Severin Housen (Sacramento: Halcyon Press, 1981), pp 38–47.

'Before They Came' and 'The Last Charge of Polish Cavalry', *Voice Free Anthology* (Dublin: Voicefree Press, 1986).

'Dialogue in Fading Light', original poem with Italian translation 'Dialogo nella luce Morente', in *L'Isola' nell Isola poesia tra Sicilia e Irlanda* (jointly published by Comune di Catania, Assessorato Alla Cultura and Universita Deglistudi di Catania, Italy, 1996), pp 32–3.

Odes to the Future: Offered to Pearse Hutchinson, contributor (Dublin: Elo Press, 1997).

'An Indian Dreams of the River', in *Human Rights Have No Borders: Voices of Irish Poets* (Dublin: Marino Books, 1998), p. 29.

'Dialogue in Fading Light', in *The Whoseday Book* (Irish Hospice Foundation, 1999). Entry for 09.02.2000.

'The Afternoons Are Mine', in *80 MPH: A Festschrift for Leland Bardwell* (Dublin: 2002), p. 41.

'Notes Towards Old Music' in *Forgotten Light: Memory Poems*, edited by Louise C. Callaghan (Dublin: A&A Farmar, 2003).

'Word Game', in *Something Beginning with P*, edited by Seamus Cashman (Dublin: O'Brien, 2004), p. 20.

'The Alter life of Books' in *Honeysuckle, Honeyjuice: A Tribute to James Liddy*, edited by Michael S. Begnal (Arlen House, 2007), p. 35.

'The Warm Stone' in *Best of Irish Poetry, 2008,* edited by Thomas McCarthy and Bríd Ni Mhoráin (Cork: Southword, 2007), p. 18.

Light Years: A Broadsheet offered to Pearse Hutchinson by his Friends on his 80th Birthday, 16th February 2007 (privately printed). Philip is among thirty-four contributors.

'Stadium' and 'Cruelty' in *Shine On: Irish Writers for Shine* (Dublin: Dedalus Press, 2011), pp 37–8.

'Daily Bread', 'Inchicore, Early Autumn 1986' in *If Ever You Go: A Map of Dublin in Poetry and Song,* edited by Pat Boran & Gerard Smyth (Dublin: Dedalus, 2014), p. 83, p. 265.

'Hamburg Woman's Song' in *Deep Heart's Core: Irish Poets Revisit a Touchstone Poem,* edited by Eugene O'Connell and Pat Boran (Dublin: Dedalus, 2017), pp 46–7.

FICTION
'The Mountain', *Sunday Independent,* 8 November 1981.

TRANSLATIONS BY PHILIP CASEY

'Ciorrú Bóthair' ("Shortening the Road") and 'An Góchumadóir' ("The Counterfeiter") by Michael Davitt in *The Penguin Book of Contemporary Irish Poetry,* edited by Peter Fallon & Derek Mahon (London, Penguin, 1991), pp 339–43 & 346–7.

'The Whistle of the Gift' and 'Last Song', translated from the Spanish of Miguel Hernandez, *Party Hat Broadsheet,* Gorey Arts Centre, Christmas, 1980.

Translation into English of original poems in Irish: 'O My Two Palestinians' (p. 25) and 'Morning Prayer' (p. 27) by Michael Davitt; 'Lipstick' (p. 153) by Liam Ó Muirthile with Con Daly; and 'For My Friend' (p. 163) with Con Daly and 'In Harness' (p. 165) with Con Daly. *The Bright Wave/An Tonn Gheal: Poetry in Irish Now* edited by Dermot Bolger (Dublin: Raven Arts Press, 1987).

'Leannáin' ('Lovers') by Michael Davitt in *Between the Lines: Poems on the Dart*, edited by Jonathon Williams (Dublin: Lilliput Press, 1994), pp 60–1.

EXTRACTS
'Work in Progress', *The Gorey Detail*, Funge Arts Centre, 1977, pp 13–6.
An extract from *"When All Fell Away"*, *The Gorey Detail*, No. 4, 1980.
A pre-publication extract from *The Fabulists* in *Soho Square Six*, edited by Colm Tóibín (London, Bloomsbury, 1993), pp 186–191.
Extract from *The Fisher Child* in *The Irish Times*, 3 November 2001.
Extract from *The Water Star* in *Writers Against War* edited by Conor Kostick & Katherine Moore (Dublin: O'Brien, 2003), pp 8–11.
'The Isle of Enchantment', an extract from *The Tins and the Pale Lady*, *ABEI, The Brazilian Journal of Irish Studies*, No. 13, November 2011, pp 13–21. Also published online at https://doi.org/10.37389/abei.v14i0.3621.

TRAVEL
Excerpt from 'Israeli Diary', *The Gorey Detail*, No. 6 (Gorey Arts Centre, 1982).

REVIEWS OF PHILIP'S WORK
THE YEAR OF THE KNIFE
'History Made Flesh', review by Patricia Sharkey, *The Irish Independent*, 6 July 1991.
Interview and review by Susan McKay, *The Sunday Press*, 14 April 1991.

THOSE DISTANT SUMMERS
Review by Padraic O'Farrell, *The Longford Leader*, 19 September 1980.

Review by John F. Deane, *The Irish Independent*, 20 October 1980.

'A Sense of Personality', review by Gerald Dawe, *The Irish Press*, 27 November 1980.

Review by Terence Maxwell of six Raven Arts publications including *Those Distant Summers*, in *The Connacht Tribune*, 29 May 1981.

Review by Sydney Bernard Smith, *Cyphers*, No. 14, Spring, 1981, pp 57–9.

AFTER THUNDER

'When Poetry Catches Fire', review by Adrian Kenny, *The Sunday Press*, 24 February 1985.

Review by Liam Ryan of ten Irish poets including Philip Casey's *After Thunder*, *The Irish Times*, 6 September 1986.

'The Raven Bag', review by Martin Conneely, *The Connacht Tribune*, 13 September 1985.

Review by J. Ardle McArdle, *Cyphers*, No. 23 (1985), pp 51–4.

THE FABULISTS

'Odd Couples', by Alannah Hopkin, *Sunday Tribune*, 25 April 1994.

Anonymous review, *The Phoenix*, 23 September 1994.

Review by Sue Wilson, *The Scotsman*, 10 December 1994.

Review by Ronan Sheehan, *The Irish Press*, 30 September 1994.

Review by Andrea Ashworth, *Times Literary Supplement*, 18 November 1994.

'*The Fabulists*, Sex and Sad Lives', review by Alannah Hopkin, *The Irish Examiner*, 8 October 1994.

Review by Sharon Barnes, *In Dublin*, 1994, nd.

Review by Eoin McNamee, *The Irish Times*, 5 November 1994.

Review by Eamonn Wall, *Review of Contemporary Fiction*, Vol. 15, No. 1 (Spring 1995), p. 182.

THE WATER STAR

Review by Patricia Craig, *The Independent* (UK), 15 May 1999.

'A Familiar Tribute from the Emerald Isle', by Stephen Harrison, *Birmingham Post*, 15 May 1999.

Review by Aubrey Malone, *The Meath Chronicle*, 7 August 1999.

'Over There, Over Here', review by John Kenny, *The Irish Times*, 29 April 1999.

Review by Arminta Wallace, *The Irish Times*, 1 April 2000.

THE FISHER CHILD

'Vivid Unravelling of History's Warped Threads', review by Dermot Bolger, *Sunday Independent*, 25 November 2001.

'The Secrets that Destroy', review by Eileen Battersby, *The Irish Times*, 10 November 2001.

DIALOGUE IN FADING LIGHT

'New Light on Old Memories', by Belinda McKeon, *The Irish Times*, 4 April 2006.

TRIED AND SENTENCED

Review by Eamonn Wall, *Cyphers*, No. 80, Autumn/Winter 2015, pp 65–7.

JOURNALISM

'Old Customs Survive in Pope's Motherland', *The Irish Independent*, 24 December 1979.

'Endearing Theme of a Modest Man', a look back at the life of Philip Larkin, *Sunday Press*, 8 December 1985.

'Philip Casey on the Success of the Oisin Theatre in Hamburg', *Sunday Press*, 11 January 1987.

'Appreciation of the Late Conleth O'Connor', *The Irish Times*, 10 June 1993.

POETRY REVIEWS BY PHILIP CASEY
THE SUNDAY PRESS

'Vision at its Best', review of *Inchicore Haiku* by Michael Hartnett (Dublin: Raven Arts Press, 1985), *The Sunday Press*, 8 September 1985.

'Recognition for a unique Irish voice', review of *The Berlin Wall Café* by Paul Durcan (Belfast: Blackstaff, 1985), *The Sunday Press*, 24 November 1985.

'Setting out his world view', review of *Antarctica* (Loughcrew: Gallery Press, 1985) by Derek Mahon, *Sunday Press*, 29 December 1985.

'Putting Kavanagh in Context', review of *The Complete Poems of Patrick Kavanagh* edited by Peter Kavanagh (New York: The Hand Press & Goldsmith Press, 1985) and *After Kavanagh* by Michael O'Loughlin (Dublin: Raven Arts Press, 1985), *Sunday Press*, 5 January 1986.

'Ripples from a Poet's life', review of Paul Celan, *65 Poems* translated by Brian Lynch and Jan Jankowsky (Dublin: Raven Arts Press, 1985) and *The Wild Marketplace'* by Thomas Transtromer translated by John F. Deane (Dublin: Dedalus Press, 1985), *The Sunday Press*, 16 February 1986.

'Poets 3 – Making Words Reverberate', review of *Winter in Meath* by John F Deane, *Age of Exploration* by Conleth Ellis, and *A Bright Mask* by Robert Greacen (all Dedalus Press). *The Sunday Press*, 2 March 1986.

'Sophisticated, witty and Sweeneyesque', review of *The Lame Waltzer* by Matthew Sweeney (Dublin: Raven Arts Press, 1985) and *The Diary of Silence*, by Michael O'Loughlin (Dublin: Raven Arts Press, 1985), *The Sunday Press*, 16 March 1986.

'Hartnett's Obsession with O'Bruadair', review of *Ó Bruadair*, translated by Michael Hartnett (Loughcrew: Gallery Press, 1985) and *Blas Meala* (No publisher named) and *The Songs of Connacht* by Douglas Hyde, edited by Brendáin O'Conaire (Dublin: Irish Academic Press, 1985), *The Sunday Press*, 13 April 1986.

'Qualities all too rare', review of *Climbing the Light*, by Pearse Hutchinson (Loughcrew: Gallery Press, 1985), *The Sunday Press*, 20 April 1986.

'Pantheon of Irish Poets,' review of *The Oxford Book of Irish Poetry* edited by Thomas Kinsella (Oxford: Oxford University Press, 1986) and *The Faber Book of Contemporary Irish Poetry* edited by Paul Muldoon (London: Faber & Faber, 1986), *The Sunday Press*, 1 June 1986.

'The poems of Coffey and Smith', review of *Chanterelles* by Brian Coffey, and *Selected Poems* by Michael Smith (both the Melmouth Press), *The Sunday Press*, 29 June 1986.

'Irish Poetry in Two Languages', review of *The Bright Wave/An Tonn Geal* edited by Dermot Bolger (Dublin: Raven Arts Press, 1986) and *The Inherited Boundaries* edited by Sebastian Barry (Dublin: Dolmen Press, 1986), *The Sunday Press*, 2 November 1986.

'First Past the Poets in 1986', *Sunday Press* reviewers on books they liked, short reviews of collected poems of Michael Hartnett, selected poems by Nuala Ní Dhomhnaill and new collections by Eiléan Ní Chuilleanáin, Dermot Bolger, Eavan Boland, Sebastian Barry, Gerard Smyth, Paul Muldoon and Padraic Fallon, *The Sunday Press*, 28 December 1986.

'Translators not traducers', review of *All things Considered* by Ulick O'Connor (Dublin: Dedalus Press, 1987) and *Unceasing Lightening* by Miguel Hernandez, translated by Michael Smith (Dublin: Dedalus Press, 1987), *The Sunday Press*, 15 March 1987

'Women Poets', review of *Selected Poems* and *Oblique Prayers* by Denise Levertov (Newcastle upon Tyne: Bloodaxe Books, 1986), *Reading the Sky* by Paula Meehan (Dublin: Beaver Row Press, 1986) and *Return Single* by Anne Hartigan (Dublin: Beaver Row Press, 1986), *The Sunday Press*, 3 May 1987.

'A Long Way Beyond Love Poetry', review of A *White Thought in A White Shade* by James Liddy (Dublin: Kerr's Pinks, 1987) and *45 Days in a Greek Cooler* by Richard Riordan (Dublin: Kerr's Pinks, 1987), *The Sunday Press*, 18 October 1987.

Review of *A Necklace of Wrens* by Michael Hartnett (Loughcrew: Gallery Press, 1987) and *Meeting the British* by Paul Muldoon (London: Faber & Faber, 1987), *The Sunday Press*, 6 December 1987.

'Broken China in Your Hands', review of *The Irish for No* by Ciaran Carson, *News and Weather* by Peter Fallon and *Poaching Rights* by Bernard O'Donoghue (all Loughcrew: Gallery Press, 1987), *The Sunday Press*, 3 January 1988.

Review of *The Arkansas Testament* by Derek Walcott (London: Faber & Faber), *Ask Silence* by Rudi Holzapfel (Dublin: Beaver Row Press) and *Road to the Horizons* by Gabriel Fitzmaurice (Dublin: Beaver Row Press), *The Sunday Press*, 17 April 1988.

'Two Poets with a Bit of Jizz in Them', review of *The Art of Life*, by Paul Durcan (Harvill Press, 2004) and *New and Renewed Poems 1969–2004*, by Brian Lynch (Dublin: New Island Books, 2004), *The Irish Independent*, 23 October 2004.

THE SUNDAY TRIBUNE

'Kinsella's Landmark', 'Blood and Family' by Thomas Kinsella (Oxford: Oxford University Press, 1988), *The Sunday Tribune*, 27 November 1988.

'Hope Renewed', review of *Mount Eagle* by John Montague (Loughcrew: Gallery Press, 1988), *The Sunday Tribune*, 16 January 1989.

'Lambasting Provincialism', review of *The Puzzle Tree Ascendant* by Hugh Maxton (Dublin: Dedalus Press, 1988), *The Sunday Tribune*, 26 February 1989.

'The Call from Within', *Poems Selected and New* by Padraig J. Daly (Dublin: Dedalus Press, 1988) and *Cicada* by

Glenda Cimino (Dublin Beaver Row Press, 1988), *The Sunday Tribune*, 9 April 1989.

'Rendering Lorca's Dance of Images', review of *The Tamarit Poems* by Frederico García Lorca, translated by Michael Smith (Dublin: Dedalus Press, 2002), *The Irish Times*, 17 August 2002.

CYPHERS

Review of Paul Durcan's *Jesus and Angela* (Belfast: Blackstaff Press, 1990) and *Selected Poems* by Phillipe Jaccottet, with translations by Derek Mahon (London: Penguin International Poets, 1990), No. 32 (1990), pp 55–8.

Review of Leland Bardwell's *Dostoevsky's Grave*, *Cyphers*, No. 33 (1992), p. 50.

INTERVIEWS

'Keeping a Comic Faith in Love', interview post-publication of *After Thunder*, *The Sunday Independent*, 3 March 1985.

'Irish Literary Revival Website Virtual Library Patrick Chapman and Philip Casey', *The Sunday Independent*, 30 April 1986.

'Rich Fantasy Springs from Harsh Reality for Philip', interviewed by Una Brankin following the publication of *The Fabulists*, *The Sunday Press*, 6 November 1994.

'Still Point of the Turning World: Arminta Wallace in conversation with Philip Casey about the background to *The Fisher Child*'. *The Irish Times*, 6 May 1999.

'If I Knew Then What I Know Now', Philip Casey is interviewed by Susan Mitchell. Topics included his childhood cancer and the Internet, *Evening Herald*, 6 January 2001.

'A Tale Told from the Heart of Emotion', Interview by Sue Leonard, *The Irish Examiner*, 23 February 2002.

COLLOBRATIONS

'Nocturnal' with Claire Berliner (London: Booth-Clibborn Editions, 1998).

TRIBUTES TO FELLOW WRITERS

Notes for His Contemporaries; A tribute to Michael Hartnett edited by Niall Hartnett (Chicago: 2009).

AUDIO TAPE

*Philomena's Restauran*t produced by Raven Arts Press, 1982. Philip Casey is one of five contributors.

OTHERS

Face to Face by Gabrielle Warnock and Jeff O'Connell (London; Trident Press, 2000). This book commemorates writers who have an association with Kenny's Bookshop, Galway through the medium of photographs. Philip's photo appears at page 43. Philip's website – irishwritingonline – is acknowledged as a source for the bio pics of the featured writers, p. 278.

16 on 16: Irish Writers on the Easter Rising, edited by Dermot Bolger (Raven Arts Press, 1988), pp 28–29, untitled contribution by Philip Casey, later reprinted in *Letters from the New Island* (1991), pp 209–210.

ONLINE REFERENCES TO PHILIP CASEY

ABEI Journal, The Brazilian Journal of Irish Studies, Vol. 13, 2011, pp 13–21. 'The Isle of Enchantment' from 'The Fins and Pale Lady' (An extract from *Coupla*), Link; https://doi.org/10.37389/abei.v14i0.3621

Mark Ulyseas; *Live Encounters,* interview with Philip Casey June, 2012, link; https://liveencounters.net/2012-2/06-june-2012/philip-casey-in-an-exclusive-interview/

Pat Boran; https://patboran.com/a-first-meeting-with-philip-casey/

Goodreads.com; nd, Philip Casey answers your questions — Ask the Author (goodreads.com).

The Parlour Review; Philip Casey – The Parlour Review, Interview with Marion Kelly.

Publishers Weekly; Review of *The Fabulists* (publishersweekly.com)

Frank Corcoran; PHILIP CASEY IRISH POET NOW DEAD WROTE THIS POEM FOR ME | Frank Corcoran.

The Stinging Fly; 1 November 2015, Extract from *The Fisher Child*, Philip Casey Archives – The Stinging Fly.

Review of Tried and Sentenced 'Tried and Sentenced' eBook by Philip Casey – EPUB | Rakuten Kobo United States.

'Climbing the Winding Stair: Philip Casey's *The Fabulists'*, *Berfrois*, 15 March 2022. Eamonn Wall on Philip Casey – Berfrois.

CONTRIBUTION TO EXHIBITION CATALOGUE

Foreword to the exhibition catalogue, *Eamonn Carter: Reconnections* (Dublin: Hallward Gallery), 20 September 2001 to 12 October 2001.

ARTICLES AND OTHER TEXTS ABOUT PHILIP CASEY

'The Paul Funge Centre has produced a Broadsheet containing the work of a number of County Wexford poets. One of the most notable young poets in the work in the Broadsheet is 20-year-old Philip Casey.' *The New Ross Standard,* 4 September 1971.

'During the festival two small books of poems by Eamonn Wall of Enniscorthy and Philip Casey of Hollyfort will be published by the Funge Arts Centre', *The Wicklow People,* 2 August 1974 and *Irish Independent,* 11 July 1974.

'Memories of a Country Priest' published in the Poetry Broadsheet by Gorey Arts Centre, a tribute to the late Father O'Regan by Philip Casey who teaches English in Barcelona, *The Enniscorthy Guardian,* 13 August 1976.

Gorey Arts Festival. It notes that 'others who will contribute include Philip Casey who teaches English in Barcelona.' *The Wicklow People,* 4 August 1978.

'Poets Get It Taped', launch of *Philomena's Restaurant* by Raven Arts Press, *The Irish Press*, 8 January 1982. Philip Casey is one of five contributors.

Poetry Reading at *Alliance Francaise* with James Liddy and Sebastian Barry for Poetry Thursday, *The Sunday Tribune*, 8 January 1989.

'Prudential Irish Schools Creative award, 6,000 entries. Judges include Philip Casey'. *Evening Herald*, 16 February 1989.

'First Gorey Gallery opens since closing of Arts Centre', Philip Casey reads 'Why I am not a Poet' by Frank O'Hara, *The Gorey Guardian*, 14 December 1989.

'*Cardinal* Will Be Presented at the International Schule in Hamburg for Two Nights Starting on November 12. *Cardinal* already Has Had a Reading in Dublin's Peacock Theatre.' *The Enniscorthy Guardian*, 18 October 1990.

'Why many Irish Poets Are Taking to the Stage' by Katie Donovan. Reference to *The Cardinal* being performed in Hamburg November 1990, The *Irish Times*, 22 January 1991.

'Waxing Lyrical with Wexford in their Bones' by Katie Donovan on the publication of *Wexford Through its Writers*, *The Irish Times*, 13 January 1993.

'Philip's Special Effort to Attend the Launch of *Wexford Through its Writers*', The *Enniscorthy Guardian*, 5 August 1993.

'Gorey-reared Novelist About to Publish First Novel.' *The New Ross Standard*, 1 September 1994.

'Philip Reader's Choice is *Cosmicomics* by Italo Calvino, *The Irish Times*, 5 October 1994.

'The Pros and Cons', Katie Donovan talks to three writers who have made the leap from poetry to the novel, *The Irish Times*, 10 November 1994.

The Fabulists is Sebastian Barry's reader's choice, *The Irish Times*, 9 May 1995.

'Philip in Line for Major Literary Award', (*The Fabulists*), notes that 'The Mountain' won story of the month in *The Sunday Independent*, *The Gorey Guardian*, 25 May 1995.

'£2,000 Prize for Irish Novel Makes Debut at Listowel. Kerry Ingredients Book of the Year award for *The Fabulists*', *The Irish Times*, 27 May 1995.

'Gorey Writer's Novel Scoops Listowel Prize', *The Enniscorthy Guardian*, 31 May 1995.

'Lamp of Welcome', President Mary Robinson's visit to Gorey, *The Gorey Guardian*, 23 August 1995. Philip's poem 'The Lamp of Welcome' was written specially to mark the occasion of President Robinson's visit.

'Philip's Novel is Translated into German', *The Gorey Guardian*, 17 December 1995.

'Author Casey to Open South Leinster Drama Festival', *The Enniscorthy Guardian*, 6 March 1996.

'Famous Wexford Writers including Philip Casey to Attend Spoken Word Festival in New Ross,' *The Enniscorthy Guardian*, 14 August 1996.

'New Ross Poetry Festival. Philip Casey Taking Part,' *New Ross Standard*, 25 September 1996.

'Forging Sicilian Friendships: Tara Hill Venue for Italian Cultural Exchange,' *The Gorey Guardian*, 11 June 1997.

The Water Star the second novel expected soon from Philip Casey, 'The Gorey Writer Has the World at His Fingertips', *The Gorey Guardian*, 30 April 1997.

'Desert Island Bookmarks', Lucille Redmond talks to five people including Philip Casey and Eavan Boland about their favourite websites, *The Irish Times*, 13 October 1997.

Colm Lambert on *The Water Star*, 'A New Novel from Casey With Strong Gorey connections', *The Gorey Guardian*, 7 April 1999.

Article on Philip's Connections with Laois, *The Leinster Express*, 29 May 1999.

'Casey's book (*The Water Star*), launched at The Mill, Craanford', *The Gorey Guardian*, 23 June 1999.

'Katie Donovan Finds Out What Irish Writers Including Philip Casey Are Reading This Summer', *The Irish Times*, 5 August 1999.

'Fabulists, Realists and the Aesthetics of Exile', review of *Contemporary Irish Fiction*, edited by Liam Harte and Michael Parker. A discussion of contemporary Irish fiction including Philip Casey, *The Irish Times*, 23 September 2000.

'Doing a Roaring Trade', seven writers including Philip Casey talk about how the boom has affected their work, Sylvia Thompson, *The Irish Times*, 10 November 2000.

'Community School to Host First Arts Week: Special Guest is Philip Casey', *The Gorey Guardian*, 13 March 2002.

'Artists Welcome to Enniscorthy Writing Weekend', a weekend of workshops including fiction workshop by Philip Casey, *The Echo*, 14 July 2004.

'Philip Returns to Help Local Kids Celebrate Monaseed: Opens Art Exhibition', *The Gorey Guardian*, 20 June 2005.

'Philip's Time in Monaseed', exhibition opening, *The Gorey Guardian*, 13 July 2005.

'When life is a Blur' by Grace Wynne-Jones, reference to *Dialogue in Fading Light*, *The Irish Times*, 23 November 2005.

'An Irishman's Diary' by Dermot Bolger, reference to *The Water Star*, *The Irish Times*, 24 November 2005.

'Out of Print, Not for Long,' *Sunday Independent*, 30 April 2006.

'Philip Casey on James Liddy as an Influence', *The Irish Independent*, 7 November 2012.

'Poets and Friends Salute a Giant of Irish Writing', *The Irish Times*, 29 August 2015.

Mary O'Donnell on the transfer of Philip's archive to the National Library, 'An Irishwoman's Diary', *The Irish Times*, 28 December 2020.

TRIBUTES TO PHILIP CASEY

'Tributes Pour in for Poet Philip Casey', *The Gorey Guardian,* 6 February 2018.

'President Pays Tribute as "Treasured Author" Philip Casey dies aged 67', *The Irish Times,* 6 February 2018.

'Remembering Philip Casey', Letter by Hugh McFadden to the letters page, *The Irish Times,* 7 February 2018.

'Not an Obituary (A gift for Philip Casey)', a poem by Heather Brett, *The Irish Times,* 24 February 2018.

'Both Tough and Tranquil: Philip Casey's Rural Childhood in North Wexford', *The Gorey Guardian,* 13 March 2018.

'Gifted Lyricist and Incisive Sure-footed Novelist', obituary by Dermot Bolger, *The Irish Times,* 24 March 2018.

'Many Gather for a Day to Remember Philip Casey', *The Gorey Guardian,* 3 July 2018.

'An Appreciation', by Eamonn Wall, *Cyphers,* No. 85, pp 52–5.

'Philip Casey in Focus', three articles by Simon Bourke, *The Gorey Guardian,* 28 April, 12 May and 26 May 2020.

Sebastian Barry, in *The Lives of the Saints* (London: Faber, 2022), pp 33–35.

From Oven Lane to Sun Prairie: In Search of Irish America, by Eamonn Wall (Dublin: Arlen House, 2019, dedication to Philip Casey).

From Gorey, County Wexford, ROBERT ARMSTRONG lives in Dublin, and is represented by the Kevin Kavanagh Gallery. He is a Founder Member of Temple Bar Gallery & Studios, Dublin and was Head of Painting at the National College of Art & Design (NCAD) until 2018. He has exhibited in Ireland and abroad and has been the subject of essays by writers including Aidan Dunne, Declan Long and Colm Tóibín. *Robert Armstrong*, a major publication by DÜRER ǀ EDITIONS was published in 2023.

MICHAEL AUGUSTIN is a German poet with strong connections to Ireland. *Mickle Makes Muckle*, a selection of his poems and miniatures, translated by Sujata Bhatt and with an afterword by Philip Casey, is available from Dedalus Press, Dublin.

From Dublin, now living in County Wicklow, SEBASTIAN BARRY is a poet, playwright and novelist. His novels include *The Secret Scripture* (2008) and *Days Without End* (2016) both of which won the Costa Book of the Year prize, and most recently, *Old God's Time* (2023). He was Laureate for Irish Fiction 2019–2021. He is a member of Aosdána.

SARA BERKELEY has published seven collections of poetry on both sides of the Atlantic. Her most recent collection, *The Last Cold Day* (Gallery, 2022) won the inaugural Yeats Society Sligo poetry prize. She lives in upstate New York where she works as a hospice nurse.

SUJATA BHATT has published nine collections of poetry with Carcanet Press, UK. She has received numerous awards. Her work has been widely anthologized and has been translated into more than twenty languages.

DERMOT BOLGER is a poet, novelist, playwright and publisher. His fourteen novels include *The Lonely Sea and Sky* and *A Second Life*, which have both recently been republished. His tenth poetry collection, *Other People's Lives*, appeared in 2022.

PAT BORAN is a poet, photographer and short film-maker. His poetry has been translated into Italian, Macedonian, Hungarian and Portuguese. His most recent full-length poetry collection is *Then Again* (2019). From Portlaoise, he lives in Dublin where he is editor of the publishing company, Dedalus Press. He is a member of Aosdána.

ULRIKE BOSKAMP is an art historian based in Berlin. She is head of a foundation for contemporary art, and co-organiser of Network Topographic Visual Media. Her last book on spying accusations against landscape artists came out in 2022. As a child, Ulrike lived in Greystones. She met Philip Casey in Dublin in 1983, and they remained close friends for life.

LORCAN BRENNAN was born and raised in Carnew, Co. Wicklow. His poetry has been published widely in chapbooks and journals.

HEATHER BRETT, poet and artist, was born in Newfoundland, raised in Northern Ireland, and has lived south of the border for over 30 years. She has published five collections of poetry and is currently arts co-ordinator with Droimín Creative, Cavan.

Originally from Clontarf in Dublin, DOROTHY BROPHY lives in Castletownbere, County Cork. For the past 28 years she has worked as branch librarian in the local branch of Cork County Library. She plans to retire early in 2024 and hopes to devote more time to her love of literature, genealogical research and her garden.

FRANK CALLERY is an award-winning poet and songwriter, journalist and social historian. Based in South Kilkenny his preoccupations are grandchildren, music and tree planting.

SIOBHAN CAMPBELL has recent or forthcoming poems in *Zocalo public square, New Hibernia Review, Crannóg* and *Empty House: Poetry on the Climate Crisis*. Her latest collection *Heat Signature* (Seren, 2017) contains poems used in commemorations of the anniversary of the Good Friday Agreement. Siobhan co-leads the MA in Creative Writing at the Open University.

MOYA CANNON's most recent book of poetry is *Collected Poems* (Carcanet). A new collection, *Bunting's Honey* (Carcanet), is forthcoming in 2025. She has been a recipient of the Brendan Behan Award and the O'Shaughnessy Award and was Heimbold Professor of Irish Studies at the University of Villanova. From Donegal, she now lives in Dublin. She is a member of Aosdána.

EAMONN CARTER is a native of Gorey. He studied art at the Crawford School of Art in Cork. He has exhibited in many group exhibitions and has held one-man shows in galleries throughout Ireland. Since the 1980s, he has been a regular exhibitor in the Royal Hibernian Academy's annual exhibition. He retired in 2011 as head of Gorey School of Art.

JOHN CASEY hails from Hollyfort in north County Wexford and grew up on a farm there. He is a retired secondary school teacher and is now living in County Wicklow.

KARINA CASEY works in CIÉ and has a keen interest in genealogy. She is currently studying for a degree in Local History in NUI Maynooth. She lives in Dublin.

PETER CASEY is a psychotherapist in private practice. Previously, he has undertaken various roles, including farmer, retailer, musician and bus driver.

PATRICK CHAPMAN's first poetry collection, *Jazztown*, was published in 1991 by Raven Arts Press. His tenth, *The Following Year*, appears from Salmon in 2024. He co-founded the *Irish Literary Revival* website with Philip.

JIM CHAPSON was born in Honolulu, Hawaii, in 1944, and educated at San Francisco State University. He has lived in Milwaukee since 1976. His most recent books are *Daphnis & Ratboy*; *Scholia*; and *Plotinus Blushed* (Arlen House, 2013). He has poems in the anthology *Jack London is Dead: Contemporary Euro-American Poetry of Hawaii* (Tinfish Press, 2013).

CHRISTINE CLEAR was lucky to know Philip from 1990 until his passing. She lives in Carlow and is completing a D.Prof in Contemplative Politics.

KEVIN CONNOLLY is the author of *Yeats and Sligo* (Brandon) and *Arise and Go* (O'Brien Press). In 1982 he founded The Winding Stair Bookshop and Café in Dublin where he hosted hundreds of literary events, most of which were attended by Philip Casey. He grew up in Bailieborough, County Cavan, and now lives in County Sligo.

MICHAEL CONSIDINE is from Gorey, County Wexford, where his lifelong friendship with Philip, John and Peter Casey began. As well as pursuing a career in law, he is a widely published poet and has an MA in Local History. He is one of the main contributors to the *Gorey 400* book.

TONY CORBETT still works as an English teacher in Barcelona, Spain. In recent years he has also been working as a translator of medical articles from Spanish to English.

PATRICK COTTER lives in Cork. His poems have appeared in the *Financial Times, London Review of Books, POETRY, Poetry Review* & elsewhere. His latest collection is *Sonic White Poise* (Dedalus, 2021).

TONY CURTIS is a Dublin poet who has read his work to acclaim all over the world. He has published ten collections of poetry and is a member of Aosdána. He was the 2018 recipient of the Lawrence O'Shaughnessy Award.

Raised on a farm near Camolin, County Wexford, KATIE DONOVAN has published five collections with Bloodaxe. Her sixth, *May Swim*, is forthcoming. She is a former feature writer with the *Irish Times* and has taught Creative Writing at iadt Dún Laoghaire and NUI Maynooth.

THEO DORGAN's most recent collection is *Once was a Boy* (Dedalus, 2023). Recent work includes writing and presenting the multi-award winning documentary *An Buachaill Gealgháireach* (2022) and the script for *Staging the Treaty*, produced by ANU (2022). He is a member of Aosdána.

Originally from Boston, ANTHONY GLAVIN has lived in Dublin for many years where he worked with New Island as a commissioning editor. He is a novelist and short story writer. His books include *Nighthawk Alley; One for Sorrow* and most recently, *Colours Other than Blue*.

SEAN HALFORD, and his wife Kay, were great and long-term friends of Philip Casey. For many decades, they have played important roles in the cultural life of Gorey as advocates for the arts.

MAEVE HICKEY is a Dublin-based artist who works in many mediums. She has exhibited widely, and is particularly known for her extensive photographic work on the US/Mexico border.

MARION KELLY lives in Dublin. She completed her doctoral thesis *Between Childhood and Night: The Role of Literature and Emotion in the Writing of Conor Cruise O'Brien* in the School of English, Trinity College, Dublin. She also hosted the podcast *The Parlour Review*.

PATRICK KEHOE was part of the James Liddy-steered Gorey poetry scene in the 1970s and early 1980s, along with Philip Casey, Katie Donovan, Mick Considine, Eamonn Wall and others. Their work appeared in broadsheets and *The Gorey Detail*. Kehoe's fourth collection, *Saturday Night*, will be published this year by Salmon Poetry.

MAUREEN KENNELLY has been Director of the Arts Council since April 2020. Before that she was director of Poetry Ireland, programme director of the Cúirt International Festival of Literature (Galway) and curator with the Mountains to Sea Festival, Dún Laoghaire.

ADRIAN KENNY is a fiction writer and translator. He lives in Dublin. He has published three volumes of memoir: *Before the Wax Hardened* (Lilliput, 1991), *Istanbul Diary* (Poolbeg, 1994) and *The Family Business* (Lilliput, 1999). He is a member of Aosdána.

BRIAN LYNCH's most recent book, *Crooked in the Car Seat*, with a preface by Colm Tóibín, is published by the Duras Press. In 2024 Duras will publish *Bury the Dust: a Zen Diary*.

THOMAS LYNCH is the author of six collections of poems, six books of essays and a book of stories. His recent books include *The Depositions: New & Selected Essays* (2019), and *Bone Rosary: New & Selected Poems* (2021). A novel, *No Prisoners*, is forthcoming from Godine. He keeps homes in Michigan and Moveen, West Clare.

CATHERINE PHIL MACCARTHY's poetry books include *Daughters of the House* (2019) and *The Invisible Threshold* (2012) with Dedalus Press. Her sixth, *Catching Sight*, and her *Selected Poems* are forthcoming. She received the O'Shaughnessy Award in 2014, and the Yeats Thoor Ballylee Poetry Prize in 2023. She is from Limerick.

DAVID MCLOGHLIN has published three collections with Salmon Poetry. He is a recent recipient of a Patrick and Katherine Kavanagh Fellowship, and featured in 2023 on the Versopolis online platform for European poets.

TERRY MCDONAGH has taught creative writing at Hamburg University and was Drama Director at International School Hamburg. He has published eleven poetry collections, as well as drama, prose and poetry for young people. His most recent poetry collection is *Two Notes for Home* (Arlen, 2022).

ALICE MAHER is a visual artist who works within the realms of nature and culture, subversion and transformation, mythology and memory. Collections include IMMA, Museum of Fine Arts Boston, British Museum, Georges Pompidou Centre, Ulster Museum.

EAMON MAHER is director of the National Centre for Franco-Irish Studies in TU Dublin and General Editor of the Reimagining Ireland book series with Peter Lang, Oxford. He has published two monographs and one essay collection (co-edited with Derek Hand) on various aspects of the work of John McGahern.

EMER MARTIN is a Dubliner who currently lives in California. Her novel *Thirsty Ghosts* (Lilliput Press) was published recently. Her other novels include *Breakfast in Babylon* (winner of the Kerry Book of the Year Award in 1996), *The Cruelty Men* and *More Bread or I'll Appear*. She was awarded a Guggenheim for her work.

PAULA MEEHAN's recent poetry publications are: *As If By Magic: Selected Poems* (Dedalus, 2020/Wake Forest University Press, 2021); and *The Solace of Artemis* (Dedalus, 2023).

HELENA MULKERNS has been shortlisted for the Francis MacManus and Irish Book Awards. Her collection of short stories, *Ferenji,* was published by Doire Press in 2016. She has worked internationally as a journalist and UN civilian peacekeeper, and for twelve years, set up and ran The Cáca Milis Cabaret, an electic evening of the arts.

AIDAN MURPHY is from Cork but has lived in Dublin for many years. His poetry collections include *Neon Baby: Selected Poems* (New Island) and *Wrong Side of Town* (Dedalus).

Born in Cork city, EILÉAN NÍ CHUILLEANÁIN lives in Dublin. She is a founder member of the literary magazine *Cyphers*, which she still edits. She has published 10 collections of poetry with Gallery Press, most recently *The Map of the World* (2023), shortlisted for the T.S. Eliot Prize.

She has been awarded the Griffin Prize, the Pigott Poetry Prize and the *Irish Times*/Poetry Now award. She is a Fellow and Professor of English (Emeritus) at TCD. She is a former Ireland Professor of Poetry.

A native of Enniscorthy, PADHRAIG NOLAN now lives near Dún Laoghaire, Co. Dublin, where he works as a graphic designer and visual artist. A limited edition pamphlet of his poetry will be published in January 2024.

EOIN O'BRIEN is a professor of medicine at both the Royal College of Physicians and Surgeons in Dublin. He is the author of *The Beckett Country: Samuel Beckett's Ireland: Conscience and Conflict: A Biography of Sir Dominic Corrigan, 1802–1880*, and *An Illustrated History of Medicine in Ireland*.

JEAN O'BRIEN's latest and sixth poetry collection, *Stars Burn Regardless*, was published by Salmon Poetry in 2022. An award-winning poet, her work is widely published and anthologised.

MARY O'DONNELL is a writer of fiction, poetry, non-fiction and essays. A limited edition chapbook was recently published by Southword Editions. Her work is translated to Portuguese, Spanish and Hungarian. She is a member of Aosdána.

MICHAEL O'LOUGHLIN was born in 1958, and founded Raven Arts Press with Dermot Bolger. He has published many collections of poetry, criticism and translations, and is a member of Aosdána.

NESSA O'MAHONY lives in Dublin. She has published five books of poetry: *Bar Talk* (1999), *Trapping a Ghost* (2005), *In Sight of Home* (2009), *Her Father's Daughter* (2014) and most recently, *The Hollow Woman on the Island* (Salmon, 2019). She has edited several literary journals and anthologies.

MARY O'MALLEY is a poet from Connemara. Her 9 collections include *Where the Rocks Float* (Salmon, 1993), *Valparaiso* (Carcanet, 2012) and *Playing the Octopus* (Carcanet, 2016). *The Shark Nursery* is forthcoming. She is a member of Aosdána.

PAUL O'REILLY's debut collection of short stories, *The Girl Missing from the Window*, is published by Doire Press. He was a member and organiser for the Launch Pad new writing initiative in Enniscorthy, of which Philip was an ardent supporter.

ROSIE SCHAAP is the author of *Drinking with Men: A Memoir*, *Becoming a Sommelier*, and the forthcoming memoir/social history, *The Slow Road North: How I Found Peace in an Improbable Country*. Born and raised in New York City, she has lived in the Glens of Antrim since 2019.

GERARD SMYTH is a Dublin-born poet whose work has appeared in journals in Ireland, Britain and the United States since the late 1960s. His most recent and tenth collection is *The Sundays of Eternity* (Dedalus, 2020).

Novelist, critic and poet, COLM TÓIBÍN is from Enniscorthy, County Wexford. His novels include *Brooklyn* (2009), which was made into a film (2015), and *The Master* (2004) winner of the International IMPAC Dublin Literary Award. He teaches at Columbia University in New York and is Chancellor of Liverpool University.

DRUCILLA WALL is a poet and critic. Her collection *The Geese at the Gates* was published by Salmon. She is co-editor of *Thinking Continental: Writing the Planet One Place at a Time (*University of Nebraska Press). She taught poetry and essay writing, and Native American literature, at the University of Missouri-St Louis until 2020.

EAMONN WALL is from Enniscorthy. His recent books include *My Aunts at Twilight Poker* (Salmon, 2023) and *From Oven Lane to Sun Prairie: In Search of Irish America* (Arlen House, 2019). He lives in the US where he is Professor of Global Studies and English at the University of Missouri-St Louis.

JOSEPH WOODS has published four books of poetry including the critically acclaimed *Monsoon Diary* (Dedalus Press, 2018). A fifth collection is forthcoming.

ENDA WYLEY is a poet and teacher and has published six collections, *including Borrowed Space: New and Selected* and most recently *The Painter on his Bike* (Dedalus Press). She is a member of Aosdána.

GRACE WYNNE-JONES is the Irish author of four highly intimate novels that have received critical acclaim. As one journalist wrote, her books are often about 'older women looking for fulfilment and, yes love, in a complicated world'.

ACKNOWLEDGEMENTS

This book would not have been possible without the support of all the contributors. The editors are particularly grateful to the Casey family, and to Shane Doyle (Philip's godson) for his computer expertise.

We acknowledge the essential support of all the subscribers to this anthology, from the USA, the UK, Germany, Australia and Ireland, North and South.

The editors acknowledge the kind permission of Vincent and Damian Casey, executors of the Estate of Philip Casey, for the use of selected extracts from the works of Philip Casey.

Eiléan Ní Chuilleanáin's poem, "The Conversation", was written in response to the editors' invitation to submit a poem for this book. Subsequently it was included in her collection *The Map of the World* (2023). The poem appears here by kind permission of the author and The Gallery Press www.gallerypress.com

Paula Meehan's poem "Letter to Philip Casey from Agios Kirikos" was written in response to the editors' invitation to submit a poem for this book. Subsequently it was included in her collection *The Solace of Artemis* (2023). The poem appears here by kind permission of the author and The Dedalus Press.

Mary O'Donnell's poem "Passion Flower on Arran Street East" was written in response to the editors' invitation to submit a poem for this book. Subsequently it was included in her chapbook, *Outsiders, Always* (Southword, 2023). The poem appears by kind permission of the author and Southword Editions.

Pat Boran's poem, "This is a Book", originally appeared in his collection *Then Again* (2019). The poem appears here by kind permission of the author and The Dedalus Press.

Nessa O'Mahony's poem, "Do Not Ask", originally appeared in *The Hollow Woman on the Island* (Salmon Poetry, 2019). The poem appears here by kind permission of the author and Salmon Poetry.

A longer version of Eamonn Wall's essay was originally entitled "Climbing the Winding Stair: Philip Casey's The Fabulists." It appeared in *Berfrois*, March 15, 2002. Online.

Katie Donovan's piece "The Night for Philip" first appeared in the *Irish Times*.

Thanks are also due to Helena Mulkerns, Rosita Boland and Martin Doyle, Books Editor of the *Irish Times*.

A special word of thanks to Alan Hayes of Arlen House, for taking on this lovely but unwieldy project and bringing it into the world for all to share.

LIST OF SUBSCRIBERS

without whom this tribute would not have been possible

The Casey Family
Salmon Poetry
Jessie Lendennie
Siobhan Hutson
Nessa O'Mahony
In honour of Deborah Troop
In honour of Paul and Ann Mims
Alan Hayes
Catherine Ann Cullen
Mark Curran
Ian Watson
Mary Shine Thompson
Ann Leahy
Nuala Hayes
Wild Honey Press
Thomas Lynch
Enda Wyley
Ulrike Boskamp
Kevin Connolly
Mary O'Donnell
Drucilla Wall
Grace Wynne-Jones
Paul O'Reilly
Heather Brett
Jim Chapson
Eoin O'Brien
Siobhan Campbell
Dermot Bolger
Alice Maher
Tony Corbett

Sebastian Barry
Eiléan Ní Chuilleanáin
Emer Martin
Theo Dorgan
Jean O'Brien
Brian Lynch
Sara Berkeley
Maeve Hickey
Paula Meehan
Joseph Woods
Padhraig Nolan
Gerard Smyth
Pat Boran
Robert Armstrong
Marion Kelly
Mary O'Malley
Tony Curtis
Colm Tóibín

Thank you, Philip